FROM ERROR TO ERROR

MONIKA KILLEEN

This is a work of creative non-fiction. While the events happened by and large in the way I describe them, I have altered many facts, names and identifying features of some characters, to protect the privacy of those whose stories are not mine to tell.

Table of Contents

To Danny

Ten thousand and one nights and counting

ABOUT THE AUTHOR

MK was born in 1976 in former Czechoslovakia. Discontented with her world shaping in Orwell's 1984 vision, she left in 1995, eventually settling in London. She learned English as an au pair and later studied law while a trainee in a city law firm. Her academic journey continued with a Master's with Merit in Classical History and later a Master's with Merit in Social Sciences.

A member of the British Psychoanalytic Council and the British Association of Counsellors and Psychotherapists, MK is a practising psychotherapist and an active campaigner for women's mental health.

Her first novel, *An Inflammable Act of Kindness*, won a Finalist Award in the Independent Author's Network Book Awards 2024.

ACKNOWLEDGEMENTS

I am indebted to the thoughtful guidance of Mike Johnson, author and tutor of mine, for his continued support on my writing journey. Mike watched over this book from its inception to its hundredth completion with encouragement and intellectual generosity.

I am thankful to Jenny Nicholls for being kind enough to agree to read the first completed version and for her magical editing touch to the manuscript before it met the world.

To Professor Raluca Soreanu, my clinical supervisor, without whose infinite capacity to share her wisdom, always surrounded by gentle patience, I would have probably never figured out too many important things.

I am thankful for the vibrant conversations with Patty Hewitt and Lauran Ivory, without which I would likely still be deciding on the book's title or its blurb. And Bob Hewitt for his clever design ideas. I hope you like the cover!

Thank you to Michelle Hooper for being the kind of reader all writers dream about and for her exacting attention to detail.

I am grateful to all those who are there to catch me when I fall — you know who you are. For all those times you say, you can do it, and eventually, I listen again.

Last but not least, to Lorenzo and the team at the Books Publishing Company. I am so grateful for all that you do!

Thank you.

PROLOGUE
1985
THE ORDINARY WORLD

It's my birthday today. I am nine. I am in the kitchen washing up my soup bowl. Dinner was the soup from three days ago. I am moving silently and fast, desperate to be out of here before he notices my presence. For my birthday present, I want to be invisible. He is cutting a slice of bread, holding the loaf precariously against his chest to steady it, slicing carefully, tongue between his lips, eyebrows bent in a frown. The knife is big with a wooden handle. He takes a weird pleasure in making it sharp, every day, he duels with the honing steel to restore the blade. Slicing complete, he places the bread on the plate. And then he sees me.

'What ya doing?' he says, although he can see.

Fuck.

'Washing my bowl,' I say, putting it down as if it was made of porcelain, not chipped old, cheap ceramic. I am trying to reach for the kitchen towel without having to get any closer to him. It's impossible, so instead I shrink myself from the inside. Holding my breath. The kitchen is small at the best of times, but it just turned into a snail shell. He is everywhere, and there is no space for me. I am up against the wall. Cornered by his madness.

He slowly turns, knife still in hand. He is right next to me now, a mad smile creeping into his face. I can feel the point of the knife touching my ribs.

'Shall I?' He asks.

'No.' I say.

'Why not?' he says, in a trance of the blade against my frozen body.

I don't reply while I slowly move from the steely point to reach for the towel. I carry on drying the bowl, I can't stop because I will have nothing to do but wait for him to get bored. He gets closer again. Knife back where it was, too close. Too close, I hear my ribs cry. I have to finish drying the very dry bowl now, I move lightly, as if there was no knife held to my small body.

'Dad. Please, stop.' The only trace of the terror that's submerging me is in the quietude of my voice.

'Dad. Please, stop.' He mocks me, he sounds demented, a small bully boy in the body of an adult.

I stand still, time stands still; we are both staring, I at the floor, he at the knife, unblinking. I don't move anymore. I know I have to let him decide when. Somehow, I know, if I try to leave, it will make him mad. And then he might. I could drown in how long it takes before he is finally bored.

Then, it's just me in the kitchen again. And, a thunder of fleeing hooves where my heart should be. I put the bowl away as quietly as I can.

This is what my father would do some days, when he was in a good mood.

CHAPTER 1
WHAT I SAID IN THERAPY FORTY YEARS LATER

I knew little about my father's parents, and nothing of his internal life. He kept it at bay from himself, as much as anyone else. I guessed it must have been a scary place because fear and darkness followed in his trail like sharks do a bleeding bait. Nothing ever felt light in his presence, and everything tottered right on the edge when he walked into the room. Thus, we all lived on Frank's edges, tiptoeing around him lest we woke the beast inside.

And then there was another Frank. One that an old family friend spoke about when she recently accompanied Mother on her big trip to New Zealand. This family friend spoke of Frank, whom she affectionately referred to as Fari — this man who was her late husband's best friend, since they were five. This Fari was a loyal friend who looked after his friend's ailing father when the friend went away to university. They never forgot how much Fari did for them, and their friendship stood the test of time. True, they didn't see him very often over the years, but once they hung out together, all the time. Roaming the neighbourhood on their bikes, doing their compulsory military service together, and there was their hobby, falconry, which has been practised in the country since the fifth century as a way of obtaining food — not as a cruel sport, the friend hastened to add.

This was a blow. It was as if someone threw my mind upside down and gave it a good shake. All the bits everywhere, I had no idea how I would put everything back in its place. I never saw this Frank. How was this possible? How was I supposed to make any sense of this? Was he two people, or did the time change him? And, if it did, then why, and did it make any difference anyway? After all, I never saw that man the friend spoke about.

As long as I could remember, I knew my father as a painfully careful man. He was careful to the point at which being careful stopped you from having any fun. His constantly furrowed forehead served as the road sign indicating a strictly no-fun-permitted entry. He was careful about all the things that could go wrong, all the things that could get damaged, except for feelings. In his world, to my knowledge, there was no "damaged feelings" category, so he wasn't careful about bashing those every now and then, including his own.

Frank was also an ashamed man, ashamed of his fear, I think, always with a shield up, defensive, angry, angry to hide the shame about being scared, about being vulnerable. Not brave enough to change things he could change, not free to leave things he couldn't. He was also ashamed in another way I couldn't put my finger on. It kept eluding me like the eye of the needle eluded my shortness of sight. He seemed fixed in a state of permanent shame, constantly on the verge of being caught doing something bad. Sometimes, if I looked at him — because I had no choice, for whatever reason — he would say, "What are you looking at? You little witch." I don't think he meant to be cruel, he just was. Maybe he felt I could see through him. Seeing him doing something shameful all the time. But he wasn't. Not if you didn't count occasionally beating up your small daughter and your wife. Which a lot of people didn't back then. Those "good old days", as they were sometimes affectionately referred to by those who dished it out and those who felt loyalty towards them, even if they knew, in their heart of hearts, those good old days were pretty messed up in many ways, and now there was a price to pay. But many saw Frank as a hard-working, scared-of-things-going-wrong man. Communism had a lot to do with sustaining fear, but there was something else, too. Sometimes I wondered if he had actually done something he felt guilty about, or was born like that. Did his parents teach him to live the life of a permanently accused man? Maybe feeling constantly on the verge of being accused made him always prepared for the worst-case scenario. After all, back then, you never knew when They might come knocking at your door. People disappeared all the time.

Frank had an old shoe box that had lived next to him all its life, the closest to his heart you could get, in his bedside cabinet. I went through it a few times, probably trying to get closer to his heart. Trying to understand the inexplicable. It seemed that some things were capable of being dear to him. That he had some warmth left in him, and it was hiding in this box.

The old shoebox contained all the seemingly insignificant little things that constituted the family treasures of Frank's ancestors and their ghosts. A few photos, some bigger than others, lacerated around the edges, sepia faded, making it hard to see what you were looking at. Much like in real life. They showed his parents and their parents and Frank with one of his siblings when he was no more than three years old. He looked bonnie and contented, but there was a look of alertness about his face that didn't fit. It seemed Frank had always been on the lookout. There were two rings, one plain gold and one silver, with the tiniest of diamonds. Tiny rings from tiny fingers, worn thin by time. They must have been women's hands that submitted themselves to these signifiers of human love that promised to last forever, but actually just died with them. Now the signifiers lay stripped of their meaning, returning to their basic property, just a bit of metal. Perhaps one day, their meaning would be restored by another hand.

There was also the old pocket watch. It was gold-plated, and it was well preserved. I had wondered how it was possible for the watch to look so pristine. Wasn't it meant to be used every day? All the time? With the tiresome job of counting the seconds of a lifetime of their owner, day in day out, timing the years going by, this watch has been passed on now three times. It was a wonder that it looked so new. And what a sharp contradiction to the worn-down rings. It was kept by a man because women didn't need to keep time in their pockets. It was a signifier of some life achievement, of a man. Different kinds of legacies. All in one old shoebox. What did this mean to him? Were they just things? Did they make him think or feel anything? He never told anyone.

Another thing that Frank was was resentful. He felt resentful about the cards he had been dealt, not able to find anything to be happy about in his entire life, at least since I was around and able to tell.

Frank had three sisters, one older, two younger. The older one left the family home as soon as she could, faster than you could say grow up. She went to university and became a professor; they never saw, first in line. I thought Kate was a cold fish who thought she was better than us. She left her family and never really came back. I guess it would be hypocritical of me to blame her for that, but as a kid, I felt she should have cared about what her brother did to my family. The other two sisters hung around and did their own thing, managing, within the possibilities of their small, oppressed town of the 1960s, to create a semblance of some happiness.

Their father was a miner. He was an ore-digger; there was no gold to be found in this old mining town. They said he was a jolly fellow. I wish I could have met him, jolly, joke-cracker-snapper, who made people laugh. My father did not inherit this character trait. Where did it go? Did it get buried in 1976 when the old man died? I can't remember my father ever making anyone laugh. Or, being jolly. It seemed a frivolity with him. A luxury not for the likes of us. I have seen him make people cry. Mainly Mother. But perhaps he was just too scared to be happy by then.

Always the bad one. That's me, eh. Always the villain. That I built the roof over your ungrateful heads with my bare hands and provide the food on the table, that's nothing to you lot. No. Just me being the bad one. Always I am the one who is bad.

To my knowledge, no one ever said to my father that he was the bad one. We were too fucking scared. Only he said it. He kept saying it every time he hurt us. There are things you don't forget. Even if you did in your head, your body remembers them. It tightens up in response to certain cues. Sometimes it's the neck, sometimes the shoulders, other times you feel it in your gut. Sometimes it can make you stop breathing for a scary moment.

Frank's mother was a housewife. Her parents did an unusual thing for their time. Independently of each other, their journey of discovery took them to mine gold in the Americas. Frank's grandmother was a bit of a dark horse. In the whiteness of the daisy-peppered fields of Slovakia, she ditched the innocence and loves-me loves-me-nots and went to America a single woman. She soon found herself with a child. It was 1905. To the extent to which the genes permitted, her son was a black man, which would have been a rare sight in Eastern Europe at the turn of that century. When she returned home, she married Frank's grandfather and soon gave birth to Frank's mother. They all four planned to return to America, but Mrs A. Merica would not have them back. Not all of them, anyway. This strange-looking family of black and white had to split to enable the son to return to where his 17-year-old heart seemed to belong, in the freedom that America offered, away from what the First World War unleashed in his other home.

And so Frank's grandmother returned, with Frank's mother, and the grandad stayed with the son until the son found his feet. Must have been a tough dilemma. Go with the wind, in search of a better life, or stay to help rebuild your war-torn little country, now that it has got its very own name, out of the shackles of the Austro-Hungarian Empire. To leave made you an unpatriotic traitor, to stay, you were a scaredy-cat. Either way, you forego an opportunity; you have to choose what you are capable of living without. I thought my father's grandfather was an extraordinarily forward-thinking and kind man, and brave to take as a wife a woman with a child not only outside of wedlock but outside the existing, narrow, cultural norms. The gold-plated pocket watch came from him.

It was in this curious history that my father's grandparents made their money, which was not inconsiderable for their time, and therefore their daughter, Frank's mother, had the luxury of a dowry which was not negligible. It suggested a life where no one needs to fear no dinner on the table. As life goes, however, her healthy dowry was no use; she wasn't endowed with good health and died when my father was only twenty-six. I was on my way then. The fact that they had an abundant foundation for living well enough also failed to provide my father with any sense of fullness. Or security. Maybe he knew that his parents were only there for a short time. Maybe when you lose your parents too soon, you will always be scared and careful not to lose things too soon. Who knows. But he feared poverty like a plague, and what is poverty but not having things? So he saved and he saved and he looked after things so hard that it was scary to be light about anything. Everything was to be taken very seriously. This way, things might never die. Like the gold-plated pocket watch. It was not a comfortable way. For him or anyone around him. Things are not meant to be forever. Having to be very careful all the time is a very tiring thing, and it is not good for you lest plague breaks loose. Frank's father died a month after I came into the world of this oppressed town, in the hot summer of 1976.

I guessed my father was likely to feel responsible for his parents' deaths in some way. It was often the case with children whose parents or siblings died in an untimely way. *"You'll be the death of me"* existed for a reason. Allowing himself the frivolity of being happy at the prospect of having a daughter was a sacrilege for which he was punished by his parents being taken away. It would explain why he could never look forward to anything again. Maybe in his mind, there was a cruel correlation between having fun and suffering. You can have fun, but not without paying the price. Perhaps, it was the last fun thing he had allowed himself to do. Maybe Frank locked his heart away in that shoe box, together with the old photos and the memories of happier times.

CHAPTER 2
A FULLY-FLEDGED HUMAN BEING WITH NO ROOTS

AUTUMN IN PRAGUE 1995

Before Leith

It's autumn and the trees' leaves do their colouring magic with the Charles Bridge cutting through the horizon, like a fine line that separates the genius from a madman. A flock of starlings is patrolling the skies above the bridge, poised perfectly, like an artist's prop, with their mesmerising aerial twists and turns and swoops and swirls. The chill in the air feels like a tease, hovering just above, not yet biting down, but I can hear its faint shrill, like a finger tracing the rim of a fine glass.

I have finished work for the day. I am walking across the bridge, hands in my pockets, heading toward the Old Town Square. I love it here, so I take my time. The bridge was the only means of crossing the river Vltava until 1841. It made Prague an important trade route between Eastern and Western Europe, and I swear I can feel its history's thunderous weight under me as my feet touch the cobblestoned ground. This city, like the bridge, has something about it. It is hard to describe if you haven't been to a place that makes you feel something good deep in your gut the moment you set foot on its ground. Your senses are absorbed, it goes right into you, gets a hold of you and won't let go until you are a part of it. Yet you don't feel engulfed or devoured. It feels just right. Like Goldilocks in the little bear's bed.

Right now, it feels like this was the moment I have been waiting for all my life. To be in charge and to be free. A fully autonomous human being. A human with no ties and no roots, a free-floating collection of atoms arranged into a shape of me, a shape that someone named Meli. I don't like many things about myself, too many, probably, and one of them is my name. It sounds like an old lady. Anyway, so far, I have not been able to discern anything about the idea of having roots "to put down" that attracts me. So far, no one has made a good case for having them. And even if it was good or meaningful to some people, it was not a village I wanted to live in. It seems to me that if you have ties, you are always bound to be at the mercy of other people's doings. Doings, feelings, misgivings, opinions. For some reason, people seem to love telling each other what to do, even if they hate being told what to do. They also seem very attached to checking in with each other about things they know to do, looking for agreement with what they think is right or sharing an outrage about what they perceive as wrong. It's all well and good and ordinary and all very boring.

At the age of eighteen, I am not looking for ordinary. The thought makes me stop and look at the thirty statues mounted on the balustrade of the bridge, petrified, watching the life pass them by. Water under the bridge. A sitting duck. Stagnant waters. Whatever analogy you prefer. To accept ties, you give up your freedom to move at will. Also, ties and lies are only one letter away from each other. When Elizabeth challenges Charlotte in *Pride and Prejudice*, Charlotte replies, "We are not all like you". She is about to accept a marriage proposal from a man who previously asked and was turned down by Elizabeth. Her point is that women might have flighty dreams of marrying for love, but most marry for security. I wonder how many women walking on the Charles Bridge in 1996 behold the same view. That was one type of a tie/lie, anyway.

There is a stone on the bridge that people travel a long way to touch. To be granted good fortune. Given how irrational humans can be, I sometimes wonder how we are still here. The "lucky" stone is part of the statue of John of Nepomuk, who was thrown from the bridge to his death. How did one man's cruel ending become a place to enable another's good fortune? I lean against the old stones nearby, feeling their cold through my clothes, to give a young couple some privacy with the stone, but not too much. I don't have all day for wishing. Looking down into the fast-flowing river, I fleetingly wonder what it would be like if the stones gave way. It's a long way. The fall would take some time. The act of falling must be nice, I think. For a few seconds, I let myself hear the wind whisper, *it will be nice, you'll see*, but when I look, what I see is a dead end, so I shut my ears and look expectantly in the direction of the young couple.

They are leaving their wishing behind now, and I stop thinking about falling and start thinking about wishing as I walk a few steps towards the place to assume the position of the supplicant, irrational human hypocrite I am. Touching the cold metal plaque of the stone, I think about all the hands that have done the same. My modest wish is that something happens tonight, something to make me feel like the act of falling might, but without the sad end. Something life-changing. They say be careful what you wish for, I think briefly, but who believes in magic anyway. I am meeting Veronika in Café Rouge, and the night is young. That is magic enough for me.

'Can you believe she has been hiding that from us?' Veronika asks me incredulously, adding 'What a squirellous bitch.'

'You know that's not a word, right?' I say.

'I'm sure it is,' says Veronika, confidently.

'Like a squirrel that is querulous?'

'Yes. Exactly. Like a squirrel who hides their nuts and is going to be difficult to confront about it.'

'And the bitch?'

'That was extraneous,' concedes Veronika, still not happy.

'Are we doing words that end in -ous today?'

'M, can we actually talk about the thing we are trying to talk about?'

'Sure, sure.' I say. Winding up Veronika is easy, a satisfying distraction.

We are in our current favourite, Café Rouge, which, misleadingly, is not a café at all. Far from it, it is a bit of a dark horse, known amongst the local folk as the philosopher's stone. It is often full of stoned philosophers, who come in the guise of students of their universities, or foreign students, and other international folk who know they will meet people in here who speak English. The enlightened ones. These philosophers in disguise who come to Café Rouge can be anything from eighteen to forty, but they are all in search of the same thing. It's like they lost something they were sure they had when they planned out their lives a few years earlier, in full confidence of their high IQs, with the primitive ruthlessness of youth. But now they were no longer sure. Things seemed better on the other side. They lost this needle in the haystack. Looking for a new meaning in their lives, they often find it in the toilets, and it looks like a fine line. An easy mistake to make.

Earlier at Café Rouge, Veronika and I found out, by accident, an accidental coincidence if you will, that our friend Beth has been hiding money from us. We saw the cash in her handbag when she went to the loo. It wasn't small change either. We went into her bag for the cigarettes that were sitting on top. This act of deceit felt weird, uncomfortable, a grave offence in the scheme of things — that edgy nature of poverty we hovered on like birds perch on power lines. Inasmuch as there were some ties in the female friendships I was prepared to take on, to a certain extent, to not disclose your earnings when the entire purpose of your being was to have fun with your friends — well, it stunk of a betrayal. We would always pool our money when it came to nights out, and Beth had just been complaining about being broke.

What is it about money that makes people weird out? At this point, it seems to be the case that it is only the people who don't have it that are capable of being honest about it. Definitely weird. It is a potent psychic currency we all hold or don't, and so much can be said about us by simply observing how we treat it. Same with our bodies and souls. I must admit, to myself only at this stage, that seeing that money had a weird effect on me, quite apart from the things I was prepared to discuss with V right now.

'What the fuck are we going to do?' Veronika says, with some sense of urgency, Beth won't be too long now, 'it's not like we can say hey what the fuck?'

'Why not?' I am confused. It seems to me like the only thing we can say.

'Well, I mean, for one, it's her handbag.'

Because I stay silent, Veronika feels she has to elaborate. 'You know, it's her handbag, and we probably shouldn't have rummaged in it, which we sort of didn't, but you know, it's still her bag and stuff.'

'And for two?'

'What?'

'You said for one. I am saying- and for two?'

'Oh for fuck sake, M. For two, it's probably like normal that she is saving some money, or something, no?'

'Normal?'

'Yeah, normal. Like you know, most people do stuff like that.'

'Guess they do.' I say, slowly, for some reason reluctant to ease Veronika's moral conundrum. 'I think what you mean is we will look like a snooping girlfriend, discovering her boyfriend was cheating on her after all. But, we weren't snooping, V. Different thing.'

'M,…' Is all that Veronika manages in response as Beth approaches our table.

The music starts picking up, and Beth sees straightaway. Her bag, the uncovered cash, the cigarettes.

'I'll go and get us a drink,' she says.

I say, 'Thanks,' and, 'Where did that come from?' I don't ask why she hid it or why she lied. Those why questions would highlight the creaks in our relationship, and now was not the time for remedial carpentry.

'Some guests left it on the bed,' says Beth, not overly explaining.

Beth is doing hotel cleaning as one of her jobs. So much for us both qualifying as primary school teachers. It seemed like a lot of money to have been left as a cleaner's tip. The Rouge is buzzing. We don't talk about Beth's uncovered secret, her exposed lie. There is a fine line between a secret and a lie. This is what comes with ties and roots, so I am not going to give Beth a hard time about it. Not much anyway. And not now for sure as the evening has promise written all over it. I can feel it in my bones. No. I can smell it. It smells like smoke.

Veronika's hair's on fire. A good-looking guy who has been looking at her all evening suddenly comes alive. 'Your hair, your hair...' Veronika turns to look at him. He is her type. A medium-height, thick-set, blonde-haired guy with an air of Grecian god about him. A small candle on the bar right behind Veronika proves yet again how small things should never be underestimated. It only takes one match to burn a thousand trees. The guy says again, louder, 'Excuse me, your hair is on fire.' She laughs, cocking her head slightly, 'What an original way to strike up a conversation'. It would look demure, until she notices my face and realises it isn't either demure or unoriginal. We all start to pat her hair frantically, until the fire is out and then we laugh because this is funny shit. We order more drinks, and now everyone has something to say.

We are on our first round of tequila shots when a group of four women and two men arrive in high spirits, seemingly also looking for the meaning of life in the same places as me and Veronika. One of the men catches my eye, or I catch his, sometimes it's hard to tell what came first, and I smile. It's almost too easy, but it never fails to deliver. It is an intravenous hit of joy, the moment in time when it's confirmed that *something you want* is going to happen, all parts assembled, in place and ready, waiting for the go signal. And it's contagious. Desire is never alone. It always has an accomplice. It starts with the eyes. They meet somewhere in the air, lock in for a fraction of a moment that is just long enough to let you know. First with a little trepidation, but soon with intent, until they spark with a promise at the margins of the night. Delicious delay. Nothing will ever be as good as this moment of anticipation. Next, in due course, it's the arms' turn. They make a move, tentatively they brush against one another, as if by accident, although nothing is unintentional in the desire that wants to get closer to another body. Cigarettes passed around, sickly shots poured down burning throats to silence the sound of doubt. The round of drinks without an end, round and round it goes. Lust tastes like tequila. It's bitter and strong, and it plays a tango with your balance.

The group is some high-level sports teams in town for a competition, and then, it is midnight, and Beth is going home. Not Veronika, not me. The party is on and also, and it offers us an opportunity to revisit Beth's betrayal. Something doesn't seem right with her, and something else eludes me about the whole thing.

'Do you think she was telling the truth?' I ask Veronika when we are briefly alone.

After a little pause in which Veronika lets her brain catch up, she says, 'I did until now,' before meaningfully adding, wide-eyed, 'Shit.'

'You don't think she is..', but her Adonis, who is called very un-greekly, Jeremy, is back, passing us both a drink.

' BRB.' He says as he disappears again to get the rest of the order.

'Selling herself? I offer. 'No. But, I wonder if..'

But then I am interrupted by an arm that winds itself around my waist and a man's mouth too close to my ear so I can hear him, 'Come and dance with us.' I look at him and smile that smile which says I see, because the eyes tell each other the rest of the story. I have sailed this sea before.

He is only in Prague for two weeks, his team is in a tournament. I didn't pay attention to what kind, except to note it was a national-level game and they were off to Atlanta next, for the Summer Olympics. It was the first Summer Games since the dissolution of Czechoslovakia, and so the Czech Republic and Slovakia competed as independent teams. All the more exciting, but you don't need too much detail. Well, I don't. I find details bring on discrepancies, and that kind of asymmetry interferes with my ideas of the next episode of my life, which I have now sketched out in my mind quite clearly, even if you only sketch using a pencil. That way, you can correct your mistakes and no one can tell.

Before I fall asleep, I remember the money in Beth's bag. Maybe she is seeing someone who is helping her out. I heard a few stories about this. There was an underground group of Albanian drug dealers around who had issues with their visas, so they would date Czech girls who would be more than happy to hang out with these older guys, be seen on their arm, in exchange for a nice pair of shoes or an expensive handbag. Maybe I should try it, I think to myself, as I drift off into a restless, dreamless, I-had-too-much-to-drink sleep.

The tall sportsman with whom I sailed into the night a couple of nights ago, I remind myself before I join him at the bar, goes by the name of Peter. He is a dirty blonde with green eyes, unshaven stubble and a good smile. His hair is shaggy, and you can see the muscles playing a game underneath his shirt as it tenses up around his arm when he raises his drink to his mouth or lights a cigarette. Maybe because he jumps hurdles for meters on end, there is a lightness to him that is contagious, but you never forget about the muscles underneath his shirt. The way he is looking at me makes me feel undressed, which, incidentally, I very much would like to be quite soon. I push the thought aside to concentrate on whatever might make my mind stop

16

playing the game with the muscles hidden by his Nirvana shirt. Apt, I am sure.

'There is something about our language that makes me nostalgic,' Peter is saying, not very rock'n'roll. We have had a few drinks now — after I finished my shift in the bar next door, where I also have had a few drinks, and he has just ordered another round. We have to sit close, the bar is full like my glass just now, and the soft jazz piece is framing the moment, improvising, pushing us closer, ostensibly because we want to hear each other, in whichever language. He is comparing the Czech and Slovak languages.

'Slovakian sounds tender. It's gentle, but it comes from the gut. It's honest. ' He says.

'Uneducated, rural, with too many consonants next to each other. Makes you sound constantly angry. Consonantly spitting angry,' I reply.

'You shouldn't speak like that about yourself.' He teases me, which is fine, and it makes me crack a one-sided smile.

I ask what he misses the most while taking a sip of my very delicious-tasting wine, thinking how wonderful the colour of it is in this light, slipping a cigarette out of the pack. Passing him one.

'I don't know. My home, I guess. I travel a lot.' He strikes the match to light my cigarette, then his, holding the same flame. He puts it out just before the flame can reach his finger. He has done it before.

He is looking for something in my face. Why do they always do this? The men I date. Just what can I get you, Sir? I toy with him, in my mind for now. I can't place what he is looking for, it is a puzzle, it is not sex. He wants me to agree with him. But that would be boring, and this isn't. I think Lacan might suggest he is looking for a shared yearning. He wants to find in my eyes what I see in his. He is imploring me with his eyes to want something he wants, while his mouth is talking about a shared language. I am ok with this.

'Why do you travel then?' The first smoke ring, always so perfect.

'I have to,' he says. What a strange question, he is no doubt thinking, didn't I hear he was on the top of his game in this sport category, I can't hold in my mind, even though he has told me at least three times.

'But do you have to? Or is it, you know, a choice? Do you not like what you are doing? Would you not miss doing it if you stayed at home instead?'

'I guess.'

'Ah. So maybe that's not it,' I say. He is probably missing his mother.

'It also makes me nostalgic for Slovenky.' He says it in our native tongue. It sounds affectionate and a tease at the same time, and he holds my eyes with his, so I know exactly the sound of the thought behind it.

'Ah,' I reply in Czech now, 'but say you meet one who refused to speak it?'

'I could still hear it, underneath,' he says. He is so close to my face now that the only thing to do is to hold my breath and try and slow my heart rate. He stays there, just for a second longer than is necessary, I feel the heat of his skin, he breathes me in shamelessly, and then he draws away, touching my glass with his, 'to Slovaks.'

'To Slovaks in the world,' I say, and I smile and think that this evening should never end. And I can't wait to get underneath the language.

CHAPTER 3
A SMALL ISLAND OFF THE NORTH COAST
OF NEW ZEALAND

2025

The transient nature of things and meeting Constance

I am in the local supermarket doing our weekly grocery shop. Against my better judgment, I decide to bring Hermione, who might only be eight, but who, from about the age of three, has days when she behaves as if she were thirteen. By some weird time-bend, such days definitely last longer than twenty-four hours. Three-going-on-thirteen-Hermione measures life in superlatives and becomes a superlative herself. Her emotions, volume, responses, mean streaks, compassion, thoughtfulness — they are all off the scale. She even makes her neat cursive handwriting either too big or too small to decipher but, it is all there, every single letter and with the little flicks and curls —like an attitude stamp. Then there are other times, which also started around the time she turned three, when Hermione turns into a wise old lady. At these times, there is some innate sense of wisdom and kindness in her aura, which I can't place as coming from me, genetically, or my parenting. So, we are quite different. Two different people. I would do well to remember that. One thing we do have in common, though, we are both scrupulously discerning about authority.

Oh, and Hermione is funny. She said she got it from her dad. While looking me in the eye, sweetly. Obviously, I think she has it from me, because Don is a dad-joke kind of a guy, unless he relaxes out of his being-a-dad-ness, which can take some doing these days.

Putting the shopping on the conveyor belt, I can see Hermione talking to a friend in the next lane of mother-shoppers in the state of almost-broken, by their kids' summer break. Hermione suddenly laughs out loud, and people around smile at the sight of the two girls. This makes me remember a scene from a restaurant a little while ago, when another group of people was amused by my daughter. That day, we were making our way through a not-so-nice dinner, sitting at a table with a view out to the sea that had no end in sight. Beautiful though it was, I like my scenery to have boundaries. Without one, it feels ominous, too big to grasp by my little mind, like a picture with no frame, spilling out everywhere and forever. Like the universe, come to think of it. Anyway, looking at the never-ending pool of water in that restaurant, I realised that while I had come to terms with my personal insignificance, it might have been more easily done in a land-locked country. The vastness of the sea without a visible frame made humanity itself feel insignificant. Interrupted in my thoughts by a weird noise emanating from somewhere very close to me, I looked back at the table, away from the sea with no limits, and saw Hermione with two potato fries stuck up her nose. She was making a peculiar throaty sound, rhythmically rocking backwards and forwards and sideways, like a solitary bowling pin refusing to fall. I'm a walrus, she explained, what's wrong?

'This is the worst place I have ever been,' Burt declared on entry, and he would have been right if it wasn't for Hermione, who could not let things be lifeless. If it took pretending to be a walrus, all the better.

I finish packing the shopping into the shopping bags, which I, for once, remember to bring, and Hermione is by my side once again. I can see something is on her mind.

'Mum, you know that lady in the supermarket?' She says as we walk out towards our parked car. Remembering where I left it is a new brain puzzle every time these days.

'Lots of ladies in the supermarket, Hermie,' I say, as I am scanning the rows of the silent cars.

'The one that was too nice.' Hermione says, like that should make everything very clear, while rummaging in her shopping bag, looking for something.

Hermione says she doesn't like it when people are too nice, it makes her feel uncomfortable. She is suspicious of things that don't resonate with her inner truth, like most people are, until they are socialised out of it. Although she doesn't know this yet, it isn't the niceness, it is the lie of it. Some people call it insincerity. But the two are the same. People who are too nice — they don't do that because they mean it. No one means to smile all the time unless the happiness is chemically induced. Mostly, I think, people lie when they are scared. It's quite simple, really. There may be complex layers to this, and nuances, but right at the bottom of this insincerity pyramid, there is a scared little boy, or a scared little girl, not wanting to be found out. People who smile too much are scared they might not be liked if they stop. They are scared that if they don't smile, people won't like them for who they are, their unsmiling selves. Scared to be true to themselves, suspicious of who they might be. I am not talking here about the genuinely nice, free-to-smile or not, people. You know those when you meet them, and Hermione does too. Maybe my own radar for dissonance in human interaction is too highly tuned. You develop this without trying when you can't be sure if one of your parents is a functioning psychotic. Not that it makes it easier to parent. Or live. Au contraire.

'Yes. No. Wait. What do you mean?' I say, distracted by a car trying to get past us.

'One. She smiled too much. Two. She put on a *squeaky* voice.' Hermione squeaks the word before she continues her indictment list. 'Three. She was talking as if she was trying to sing. Not like good singing. Really annoying kind of singing. Like when Burt sings. She was just too nice.' Hermione pauses to give weight to her charge of Indecent Exposure of Insincerity of this shop assistant, who indecently exposed a part of herself in a manner contrary to Hermione's standards of appropriate behaviour.

'Well, I think that sometimes…' I attempt to put forward some mitigating circumstances, but Hermione is not finished yet.

'I don't think people are meant to be too nice, Mum. People should just be friendly, or they can be bad-tempered, like the ladybird, remember? But this lady was neither. She was just too much of a nice. Which you can't even say properly because it is not a proper way to be.' Hermione rattles on, gravely yet pleasantly, completely unfazed by the movement of the life around her, easily taking it into her stride, she strides as she speaks.

'Yes.' I can't mitigate now, the charge more complex than it was a few sentences ago.

'Yes, what, Mum? Do you agree with me?' Hermione says.

She briefly stops to make a point, which is that she is waiting for more than one word in answer to her thoughts.

'Yes, I agree, but don't go around saying Mum doesn't like nice people, ok?'

'Mum, do you think it is better to be too nice than bad-tempered?' She asks a good question, ignoring my only half-joke.

'What do you think, Hermione?'

'I don't know, but I prefer bad-tempered to too nice.'

'Me too.'

'You can always walk away.'

'Well, sometimes you can't. But that's another story.' Argh, I immediately regret saying that, knowing this will open up a wormy can. Why do I always have to tell the whole truth and nothing but the truth?

'Tell me it.'

'Not today. Another day when you are not eight, ok?'

'I am practically nine.'

As I put the last bag of shopping in the boot of the car, I briefly reflect on the times I could not walk away. Not from my bad-tempered father. Or, Daniel, the bad-tempered flatmate in Prague. Or the bad-tempered supervisor in London. A few other times, one of which I forbid entry to my consciousness, when I could not walk away from men who were in a position of some authority over me, who were either bad-tempered or a variation of it. And there are other things I still can't walk away from. They seem to go everywhere I go, although often their presence is silent. It gets louder when my mind is thrown a curve-ball, unexpectedly, usually in the form of hearing a man shout in the street, or a child being handled harshly in a supermarket, dogs being yanked by leads too hard, seeing kids crying, seeing Burt crying, thinking people hate him. Then the presence gets a voice, and there is nowhere I can go to get away from it. I know it's him. My father's voice, internalised and at the ready to make me feel small and hopeless once again.

I slam the car boot shut, a full stop on the thought, or so I think. I walk around the car when I notice Hermione still standing there, arms folded, waiting.

'Oh. You are still here. Well, when you are practically nine, for example, you might not be able to walk away if your dad is a bad-tempered man. Now, can we please go and sit in the car to continue this conversation?'

'Why can't you? Why not just go to another room?' Hermione asks as she walks around the car, opening the side-passenger door, sliding in like she is weightless.

'He might not let you. Or, there might not be another room.' I say, as I lower myself with a groan. My arthritis is killing my back, slowly but surely.

'That would suck. But why wouldn't he let you?'

'Because he is bad-tempered and he wants to take it out on you.' *Or, because he is dangerously ill and thinks it's fun to make you feel scared.* We close the doors at the same time. It sounds like ta-dah. Bang, bang.

'That's more than bad-tempered, Mum. That's holding you a prisoner. Like Rapunzel was. By her evil step-mother.'

'How do we know she was evil?' Sensing an opportunity to redirect the conversation, I jump on it. I am not sure how much of the truth Hermione is ready for. How much truth am I ready for?

'Err… Because nice-mannered people don't lock people up in a tower to stop them from having a life with their prince.'

'What if she was just being protective? Maybe she just wanted to wait for Rapunzel to grow a bit older so that she would be better equipped to deal with bad-tempered people?'

'I have no idea what has got into you, Mum, but you are getting very confused about kids' stories.'

Was my father trying to protect me? From some danger he perceived in his unsound mind, tortured by the oppressive fear that held our Communist society prisoner like an invisible straitjacket?

'You are right. And I need to concentrate on reversing out of this carpark. We don't want another near miss which you will translate to Dad as "Mum practically hit the post" now, do we?' I smile at my daughter.

'Wanna crisp?' Hermione offers her little hand still covered in arts and crafts remnants from her afterschool club, and when I nod, she unceremoniously plops it in my mouth. 'Better?'

I never heard of this place until six months ago, when we saw it on a reconnaissance trip to New Zealand during the kids' UK summer holiday. We didn't plan on coming here. We went on a detour to visit an old friend of Don's, Martie. Navigating the meandering roads of this small island hidden in the deep, lush bush like a good secret. Don said, "I think I could live here."

Martie told us the island used to be a hippy paradise. Beaches galore, trees, trees, trees and more trees everywhere, their curved arms reaching for the skies, birds fearless of men who loved their song. Lots of arty folk, doing their own thing, lots of funny things to smoke, no violence and tolerance of one another's differences as vast as its residents' cultural and economic backgrounds. London has nothing on it, Martie said. Just wait and see. Let me show you.

Is it safe, I asked Martie on that trip six months ago. Pah, is it safe. If you don't behave, the police will escort you to the mainland, and your route back is the Bermuda triangle, he said.

Martie also told us the island had two police officers and no crime to write home about, given the real, actual-life ostracizing. The last murder on the island was nearly thirty years ago. The most common report in the local weekly paper was of drink-driving. Which was on the money, 'because a lot of folk drink-drive here and everyone knows it, so everyone is extra careful. It works. Most of the time, obviously.' He said with a big smile on his face. Oh, and did I tell you, he said, there are thirty-six vineyards on the islands' thirty-six square miles.

That first night Martie took us out, he said we were going to a bar. He said it was a bit of a hidden gem and asked me not to put it on social media. Just wait and see, he said. So we waited and we saw. It was someone's living room, with a small bar installed and homemade beer on tap. The beer was good, as was the company. There was a scientist, a journalist, art people, mad people, sad people; there were poets, writers, professors, bus drivers and local politicians. Also, children and dogs. And it all worked together in a refreshing, simple way.

Many of the island people have moved here in the last ten years or so. They could be from anywhere. Many were in culturally mixed partnerships, and because everyone was mostly other, no one was bothered. The island had a lot going for it.

On the other hand, Don and I lived in the UK for twenty-six years, and sometimes twenty-six years is enough. It was longer than we had lived in our own countries. For both of us, England was a far cry from the country it was when we first arrived, separately, from different parts of the world, to the whirlwind of the Labour victory and the promise it brought with it. It was a long time ago now, and it wasn't just the country that had changed. We have all become a bit more conservative in our ways, although in my case, being "more conservative" didn't actually mean I was conservative at all. Just a little less up front. In addition, along the way, we also gathered two small humans who, since their early days, knew what Martin Luther King did in 1963 — there is power in unity and there is power in numbers. The kids were intractable and always ready to plot the next attempt at parental coup d'etat. They do slow you down, like it or not, so you might as well try and like it. And, a dog, obviously. Even though a few years back I said over my dead body. Turned out Pooch was one of the best things that ever happened to me. All she wanted was to love everyone and be frequently fed.

Once we decided, there was no dithering. Don and I are not ditherers. When we told our friends and family, they said things like, What a big move, a big decision, guys, you are so brave. I would nod — who doesn't want to look brave, but later at night I would think, were we though. 'Are we brave, Don?' I would ask him. He would say it was a big move, but it would be great. Don, the Normaliser. But I agreed. We had each other, and we were making a decision to change the route of our journey out of choice. We were not hitchhiking, we were driving this thing. I have done braver things. It was true, I was worried about the children. They were settled in their little lives, carefully contained by the English countryside, in the bubble we made for them.

Back in the car, on that trip six months ago, I replied to Don, 'So could I, I suppose,' feeling a familiar buzz in my stomach. And that was that. Because some things override all things, sometimes, it is the buzz in your stomach that makes you do things.

'Are you scared?' Flitwick asked me.

We were walking Pooch, and the departure time was only a few weeks away.

'I don't know. I don't think I have any time to be scared because everything is so busy,' I replied.

Selling a house, packing a house, having two children and a dog, and being a psychotherapist created a schedule that permitted little time for exploring one's feelings.

'I will miss you,' Flitwick replied.

She was sad, and I felt bad because I was not feeling sad then. It wasn't that I wasn't going to miss my dear friend. It was just that I was too excited to feel sad. The possibility of something new happening always brought a tremor of nervous excitement. I was like a kid the night before Christmas Day. I questioned myself, of course, why was I leaving again?

It made me think of Mozart's Don Giovanni's list. Contrary to how it looked, Giovanni did not get much pleasure from his many sexual conquests. Making the list was where the jouissance resided. It was the list of his mistresses that was his master. I wondered if my master list was my apparent inability to be satisfied with what I had. Always in a latent search for the next possibility, I was probably never happier than when one was on the way. These came and went, and some stayed, but the thing keeping me going on being was the understanding, or hope, that there was always more. That there was more to life still. That there always would be more to it than what has just been.

'I will miss you, too.' I said to my friend, because that was true. I would miss Flitwick so much. Flitwick could make me laugh. Laugh out loud and laugh a lot. We would laugh so much that we would often laugh ourselves to tears. It was so good for the soul. Flitwick was so good for my soul.

Dostoyevsky said that freedom was in being. He said, if you want to be happy, be. But *being* was not so easy some days, never mind being happy. Also, freedom could be paralysing. The more freedom one had, the more difficult being could become. People were used to boundaries, including on their freedom to be. More than used to, they came to rely on them. That's how dictators ruled — a lot of people lived by being told what to think and what to do, and they wouldn't have it any other way. So, freedom required a level of sophistication and an acceptance of the fact that life was overall fairly depressing. Embracing the fact that life was not fair, or even that it was fairly unfair. And that no matter your decisions, it was all going to end one way. That the only freedom you had was in your head. And good luck finding it.

At that point, six months ago, when we were sitting in the car, parked up outside our rental house, Don looked at me with a question in his face and in his mouth, a question that was all over him, 'Are you sure?'.

'Yes, let's do it.'

I didn't want time to think about it. Thinking time raises all the options and the necessity to evaluate each of them. Then you end up making a tortured decision based on elaborate calculations, assessing the advantages and disadvantages, as if life were an accountancy riddle.

'I think we should do it before Christmas.' Don said, and this was also a question.

That gave us three months.

'Yes, I think we should.' I answered.

And so we returned to the UK, sold our house and moved to New Zealand before Christmas. A twenty-six-year-long chapter of our lives done and dusted. All it took was one drive around our new neighbourhood. This is how one detour can become your yellow-brick road.

Yes, I would miss Flitwick terribly. But you can't have everything. Often, you leave some of the best things behind, knowing, hoping, they will always be there when you go back. Knowing that you will go back. From time to time. Because life is about time to time.

Back in our kitchen, I unpack the shopping while Don is busy fixing the spotlights on the ceiling. 'Is there anything wrong with them?' I ask, putting some beers in the fridge. First things first. There is nothing wrong with the lights that I can tell, but I never look at things that closely, partly because I am almost completely blind and partly because it isn't important to me unless it is. As the lights are in a perfect working order, there is no reason in the world that would make me look at the things close up. That is for moths. And Don.

'Yes, they are not efficient lightbulbs, and also, they are not placed properly. Also, the wiring circuit is going to have to be changed...'

I stop listening. It's too much information of the kind my brain simply refuses. I don't mean to stop listening. It just happens.

Don loves to look at things closely. He loves, possibly more than anything else, to take things apart and put them back together. This is what he did with me. It was a twenty-year project that one, and still going. A bit like Sagrada Familia, and Don has the patience of a saint when it comes to making things work.

'That sounds quite involved.' I say that because it sounds like it might fit.

'Ah, yeah, it is a big job, but it needs to be done. It will be so much better,' Don says and grins. 'Well, done, duckie. Good pretending at listening.'

I smile and say, 'It's the least I can do.'

Taking things apart and putting them together again puts you in a unique position of knowing exactly how things fit, what makes them work and what makes them creak. Don took me apart, like a million-pieces jigsaw puzzle, although a car engine might be a better analogy with Don, bit by bit, gently and carefully over the years, scrutinising each component, examining its deficiencies and proficiencies, and then, taking the utmost care, putting all the parts back in, having cleaned off the rust.

Millions of repetitions of the same thing. Countless iterations of you can trust me to never hurt you. That was the thing. You really have to build trust. Tiny bit by tiny bit. But it wasn't easy. Because my template for men did not fit. And I had had too many repetitions on that, too. But when I married Don, I gingerly let myself believe in love for the first time in my life. That was twenty-seven years ago.

The first time I met Constance was at a community hall where the locals came together once a month.

'We need to get there for five,' Don said, 'and be out by seven. Seems strange.'

They were strict about this time boundary at the Hall. BYO and be out by seven, which suited me well. Early drink, early bed. I have firmly arrived at that age when your bed becomes your best friend.

'Well, I guess there is only so long you can talk about the dead and the divorced, or how you are going to decorate your letter box in the competition,' I said to Don as I passed him the car keys. But I liked it. There was something warm and homely about this community, which, despite being close-knit, would stretch itself each time to make a room for new members who showed interest in their lives and way of living.

Constance was the daughter of a culturally mixed couple. She was certainly neither black nor white, and nothing was, the way Constance looked at things. She spoke quietly and fast, like she wanted to disappear into the canvas. She wore well-cut, beautiful dresses that spoke about her more than she ever would. Like the feminine dresses out of the 1950s, suggesting submissiveness, compliance, femininity, uniformity, likeness for a frame, or a form, hiding well the complexities that lie underneath it.

It seemed to me that Constance was built on contradictions. She was distant, yet I felt close to her. She had an unassuming manner, yet there was some deep wisdom in her. I was fascinated by her and almost instantly decided I would love to become friends with her, if possible.

A few of us went back to ours after. Those of us who didn't like to parenthesize our time by a Memorial Hall. Me and Constance sat outside, and smoking one cigarette after another we talked about being mothers, wives, friends and on the outside of the circle. Also, about giving up smoking. Like the penguins that huddle together to keep warm in the storm, you need that outside loop for it to be a circle, for it to be a thing complete. Some like it hot, right in the middle, others prefer to be away from the epicentre because it gives a more comprehensive vantage point. Although you might not be as warm.

That night, we talked about many important things, but we also held back. Naturally, but you can always tell a thing that's somehow most important — or most tricky, and most important only because it remains unresolved, because of its absence in a piece where it belongs. Huddled on the outside of the circle of that night, we didn't talk about being daughters of our fathers.

Because shame stops people, even if it isn't ours to bear.

CHAPTER 4
WHAT I DID IN THE WINTER OF 1995

PRAGUE

To be or not to be, with child, that is one question

A zygote is a cell formed by a fertilisation event between two gametes. The zygote's genome is a combination of the DNA in each gamete and contains all of the genetic information of a new individual organism. I am reading in a worn-out-looking book — perhaps, a reflection of its subject matter. I am in the *Clementinum*, the city's second-largest building. It's intimidatingly large, and it has the gravity of an old schoolmaster. Everyone here whispers, half-expecting to be told off. This is my kind of church. I came here today to educate myself on the state of my uterus. In the embryonic development of humans and other animals, the zygote stage is brief and is followed by cleavage, when the single cell becomes subdivided into smaller cells. I am trying to explain to myself that what I am about to do is ok. It is ok and it is not a murder.

Next, I get lost in my thoughts, lost in the *Clementium*, lost, just lost and at a loss for what to do.

This was the point in my life when I could have ended up like my mother. Not yet twenty and pregnant. With a man I had sex with when that would be the only true thing we would ever have together. The rest of it was more like a role-play, trying out a way of being with another, as if it were an outfit. It was fun, but I was fairly sure this was not a solid basis for a lifetime partnership. Or parenting. Anyway, I was eighteen and I found myself in a role I was not counting on. I could have a child in a few months. Half-Middle-Eastern, half-European. What would that make them in the eyes of my racist little hometown, my small-minded, scared-of-things-going-wrong family; what kind of a life could I give them? And myself. I was not going to wait to find out.

It was a knotty thing, though. I was a girl with no roots, yet there was something inside me that had its roots in my very core. Did I have any right to uproot it? To cut off its only lifeline?

It would be ok, but I had to be quick. My uterus so far contained only an encoded set of instructions localised in the forty-six chromosomes. But I could feel it, *the ordinary cell proliferation by divisions*, the early building units for the future organism. I could feel it, and it was a big knot to untie.

A bunch of cells. Just a bunch of cells, I told myself for the hundredth time and still I could not hear it.

I watch him walk up to the bar, seeing the side glances of other women, checking him out. Leith is hot. If he was a horse, he would be that jet-black, shimmering stallion, tall, proud, restless, always the favourite with the bookies. I like looking at him when we talk, and it feels good that I am the one sitting with him in this bar, not some other girl. Leith is also a bit mad. It's only a tiny hint of insanity, and that makes him also feel like a horse that could rear up and throw you hard. But that isn't what Leith does with me. Leith means lion in Arabic, and my star sign is Leo, so, obviously, I feel we are profoundly connected in spirit. We do get profoundly connected in other ways also, and spirituality has little to do with that. When I listen to him speak, it makes me think of an orchestra playing Bach's symphony. The notes hit and seduce, they lull and tease, and transport you to a place you haven't been. Orchestrated just for you, you can't help being drawn in, and you happily get caught up in it. It is art and it is a thing of beauty, but it is also not real life, and despite our lionesque connectivity, I know this. We have sophisticated conversations about things that don't matter or mean too much, because we are not trying to change anything. The only thing we are trying is to impress each other. With our words, with what our minds can do with our words, like artfully fencing swords. It's a seductive dance, the crescendo before decrescendo, while drinking cheap red wine and smoking too many cigarettes.

'Did you see that?' he says, as he puts the drinks on the table between us.

'What?'

'That couple over there. I think she just broke up with him.'

'How?'

'She gave him his key back.'

'She could have been giving him her key.'

'He didn't look like someone who was just given a gift of a promise of a future together. He looked like one was taken away from him.'

I look in the direction of the couple and I see it. The man is looking at the woman, the woman is looking down, picking off invisible dirt from behind her fingernails. What is she picking, I wonder. Is it the DNA of another man?

Remembering how the guilt that you might be hurting someone feels oddly good, I say, 'Sometimes, you have to, maybe.' It's the familiarity of the punishing principle; guilt is deserved, no matter what.

'Return a key or take away a promise you made?' Leith asks with a look I can't quite identify.

'Return the key.' And then I say, 'Did she make one though? She could be doing him a favour. Are you saying she should not have accepted the key in the first place?' It is getting late, and I don't want to talk about the couple anymore. Or keys and toothbrushes. I don't want to talk about anything anymore.

'I'd say so. If you accept the key, you accept the new terms and conditions. Someone is giving you access to their world without you having to knock first. Trusting you to walk into it, not disturbing it. It's the next step after the toothbrush.'

Now I know I don't want to talk about it because I don't know what I would do with a key. I just want to go to Leith's now, he can unlock the door, I am quite happy with the current terms and conditions.

When we later sit on his bed, looking through the CDs, choosing the right one, there is a comfortable sense of quiet expectation about how things will go from there. I light us both a cigarette and I take off my coat, absentmindedly, arm by arm, throwing it over an old chair that can't take much more than a coat. There aren't many things in this room. The chair next to the single bed, an old chest of drawers with an ashtray where other people might have a pretty vase. Or a potpourri. A single stand-up wardrobe and books. Books everywhere. On the floor, on the bedside table, by the fireplace that no longer serves a purpose other than as a book holder. Sometimes a book pile serves as a side table, to hold a glass of wine and an ashtray closer to bed. I switch off the main light and flick on the bedside lamp. Leith sometimes shares his flat with Daniel. He is also a journalist, just significantly madder than Leith. Although Daniel has his own flat, he doesn't like being alone with himself, so he is often here. I had rented a room in Daniel's flat a while ago, which was how I came to meet Leith in the first place. I owed Daniel more than some rent. Despite, or perhaps because of his madness, Daniel kind of saved my life when I became homeless once, very late at night. And then he gave me Leith.

Leith and Daniel work for the same Arabic newspaper, based in Prague's city centre. Daniel has been here for over thirty years. His Czech is flawless, which is close to a miracle given the difference between Arabic and Czech languages. Daniel is in one of his moods tonight, and he is playing a guitar, too wide awake to go to sleep. He is complexly wound up so tight that sparks around him are almost tangible through the wall. Leith gets so mad about this.

'He is doing it so that we don't forget he is here. He doesn't want us to do anything without him. He is like a child. Stupid adult who acts like a child.' He spits the words out this time. Short. Sharp. Punctuated, you feel the exclamation mark.

'Daniel,' Leith addresses the wall, shouting in Arabic, 'get out.' I love hearing it. It is so lively, this language, it is like a whip, and then it is a song. Daniel shouts something back, and Leith translates, he is so curiously polite in some ways. 'He said he would stop now. Are you ok?' He asks me. I nod into his warm shoulder. 'About him being there?' He clarifies, as if I didn't understand, that's what he was asking me. So I nod again. I couldn't care less. There is a whole wall and a closed door between them and Daniel. As far as I am concerned, he could be in another galaxy. All you need to do is close the door of your mind on it. Swing, slam, pull, creak, click.. gone.

Leith is continuously intrigued by me. I can tell this. I am not like other white girls he has been with. Other white women he has dated. I match his madness and free spirit, and he loves what we do when the lights go out, and sometimes they don't. I am single-minded about sex, like you might expect a man to be. I know he doesn't love me. I don't love him. I am also intrigued. We are two people intrigued by each other. Respectful of each other's madness, testing each other's sanity and freedom boundaries, trying to make sense of things that are different. Different skin colour, different smell, different cultures, both plucked out of our own tribe, not feeling like we belonged. This is the thing I find a common denominator in life; always an outsider, always on the outer edge of the circle, the odd one out, but you are not alone on the outskirts. You find your people. Soon we drift off to sleep, content enough, not alone and not lonely, for now.

'Leith, it's me.' I say into a very cold public telephone receiver. It is minus eight degrees Celsius. Much like my heart feels today.

'Hi, you ok?'

'There is something...'

'Yes?'

There is a pause. I really do want to tell him, but something stops me.

'Something I need to tell you.'

'Ok. I can wait,' he says. He means, on the line.

'No,' my mind suddenly made up. 'I will see you at seven, usual place?'

'Ok.' He says, and then 'M?'

'Yes?'

'I got you a toothbrush,' I can hear a smile in his voice. And an expectation.

'Oh,' I say.

'Ok, see you then.' He puts the phone down quickly to hide his disappointment. He is proud. More than anything, Leith is proud.

I wasn't there at seven. I decided I wasn't going to tell him. Not before I got rid of it, anyway. I could not let myself think about it in any other way than that. Not the beginning of a human life, growing inside me. No. Just an "it". A mass of cells. There was no way I could end up like that. With a child, before twenty. With Leith.

It was devastating in the end. My body just didn't want to let go of the promise of the life inside its womb. To expel it did not go as expected. I was thrashing around so much that I fell off the operating table during the procedure, even though I was knocked out on the anaesthetic. They kept me in the hospital for an extra few days to keep an eye on me. I hit my head when I fell, but that hurt the least of all the things that hurt.

My friend, Veronika, comes to pick me up from the hospital. We will take the metro, but at least I won't be alone. I have not called Leith because I can't face it. He will understand my decision, I am not worried about that. Also, I am not worried because I am angry. It was an accident, yes, but I can't see him again. Not like we did, and there was no point in seeing him in any other way. I am angry with him, angry that this sort of thing happens to a woman. There are no consequences for men, not physical ones, anyway. They will never have to feel the thing inside them, then the guilt inside them, the doubt that could drive you mad. But I have to stop being angry; something is wrong.

'What is it?' Veronika says as I lean against the chilled wall of the underground station.

'I can't walk,' I manage to whisper. 'It hurts too much.' I faint shortly after that, and the next thing I know, I am on an ambulance stretcher being nee-naw-ed back to the hospital. Veronika is with me, sitting in the chair next to the stretcher, worry making her face look older and wiser than her usual grinning fool-self. 'Are you ok?' she says gently when she sees me come to.

'Yes, I think so.' But I'm not. The only thing that is better is that I am lying down. The pain in my abdomen is tearing. There is a burning stone in my womb being thrown around to the rhythm of the ambulance bouncing off the cobbled streets of Prague's city centre.

'They think the procedure might not have been completed properly,' Veronika says very quietly. As if by keeping her voice low, she can keep out the terrible, grotesque truth of the present situation, which is that there is still some part of the human to be, decapitated in my womb, not fully removed with the rest of its to-be body.

I close my eyes. I want drugs. I want anything not to have to think about it. And then an idea starts to form itself. Of course, I think this is the thing to do. All I have to do is leave. I open my eyes, and Veronika says, 'What is it?'

'You know that girl in Jojo's who was talking about going to London to be an au pair?'

They are pulling up outside the hospital now.

'Svetlana, yes. What about her?'

Being lowered in the stretcher carefully out of the ambulance, I say, 'Could you get me her number?'

'Yes, M, but why?' And then, 'Oh M, don't.'

Veronika is walking next to me on the stretcher, and the two paramedics are pretending not to be listening.

'I have been thinking about it for a while. Maybe this is a sign.'

'Err...' one of the paramedics clears his throat, 'someone will be with you very shortly.' They walk away and leave us in the room, outside the operating salon.

'It is only a sign if you want it to be a sign.' Veronika says, and then changing her mind about signs, 'It could be a sign you should settle down?'

'Are you crazy?' I say, suddenly fully on, despite, or maybe because of, the pain. 'With Leith? Sure, that should work out like a dream. Black and white one. And, thinking about it, why don't I bring him home to my white, slightly racist parents in our white town, where everyone looks down on the local Romani like they are another species of animal? And then find a shitty job and work with people who are happy with shitty jobs in a small town with even smaller-minded people who have no clue that there is a life behind the thick walls they have put up around themselves because they are too scared to try anything new?'

Then, before I can finish, the door opens and Veronika is asked to leave and wait outside. I am pushed in and knocked out once again. The drug-induced heaven of blissful not-knowing.

'No, you could stay here, M.' Veronika says to the closing door, stubbornly, shaking her head.

I am not right to not open up my mind to other ways of being. That's what Veronika is thinking. Other ways than running away every time something comes up that challenges my worldview. Veronika knows that it feels scary for me to imagine I could have a good, ordinary life. That I deserve a good, ordinary life. She knows because I told her when I was high.

As I drift off to the temporary heaven, I am thinking, I've been doing too much floating, too much headlong first. Too much directionless pivoting, right on the edge of reason. I need to take stock. If I don't sort it out, my newfound freedom was only good to drown myself in. In which case, I might as well be going back home.

Veronika brings that girl's phone number the next time she comes to the hospital. There is no point in arguing now. Leaving is a thing I have a lot of practice at. I am a proficient leaver. Leaving things always carries a promise of something new. Why wouldn't you leave is not even a question, half-formed. Because I am not either. Because when you are fully grown up, you don't run away. You face things. You look things in the face and say ok, let's have a look at you.

This was the point in my life when I could have ended up like my mother. Not yet twenty and pregnant. But I didn't because my mother kept her baby. And had she not, I would not have a single story to tell. Reconciling a lifetime of anger with a lifetime of gratitude is a lifetime's work.

We get off the metro and walk the short distance to the International Coach Station. I can't afford to fly. I am with my friend

Emile, who is carrying my bag for me. I am still a bit fragile from the procedure. "Procedure" is how I think of it now, and the procedure is now in the past. Door shut, lock on. I am glad Emile is here. His unassuming presence is exactly what I need to take me through the threshold of these two places, the threshold between the now and then. Emile mainly looked after me since we first met in Jojo's that night. But he couldn't always be there, obviously. I looked like an adult, so I had at least to try to play one. Anyway, Emile gave me his old hockey-kit bag to pack all my things in. It was at least twice the size of the bag I had when I left home. Emile was a good player and a good friend, he said he would get another one.

I return my mind to my body in the street, walking on, hearing Emile say, 'Keep in touch, M,' and 'be careful.'

'I don't know if I know how to do that, Emile,' I smile. He says, You have to try, promise. And I promise because an unwanted pregnancy is a thing worth making a promise over. Because it is not an easy thing for a woman to decide she will not keep a baby. It is a huge, momentous bunch of dark clouds that will forever stay at the back of your mind, threatening to break into a thunderous storm of how-could-you and why.

'I have about twenty-four hours to think about it,' I say to Emile, 'maybe it is enough to think about all the ways in which I can be careful.' I smile at Emile, feeling suddenly hopeful. And then I come to a halt. 'It can't be! Can it? It is. Oh for fuck sake, Veronika.'

Leith is at the station. Apparently, he is waiting for something.

CHAPTER 5
LONDON COVID AND BEYOND

2020

The Economies of Home schooling and being a Rapunzel in your fifties

Everyone is crying. Everyone was screaming just a minute ago, but now everyone is crying. Everyone except Don. He is talking to his employees in a meeting on Zoom, looking crisp and sharp, matching his snow-white shirt, and completely unfazed.

I can hear him laughing from behind the closed door, and it is possible I might combust and implode, like an inward-facing volcano erupting on my inside. So, in an attempt to save myself an ulcer or two, I imagine instead breaking down the white wooden door that stands between me and Don on his call in his white shirt. I see myself going in there with a giant axe, smashing up everything in sight, and the thought makes me feel better. Not much, but it will have to do. It is as though the last fifteen minutes did not happen in Don's universe. And because he is calm, I have to carry the madness that surrounded us all only a short time ago because someone has to. It doesn't just evaporate. The last fifteen minutes were when everyone was shouting. Both kids needed a laptop or iPad and their school login to work, which they wouldn't, and there was the inexplicably pressing deadline of time when their teachers were going to greet them and welcome them to this new hell that was an online class of twenty or so five-year-olds. That was Hermione's class. Then there was Burt, who was having to register at exactly the same time, who thought this would be helpful? – followed by a maths class with his form tutor. I have a new client to see in less than an hour. My new business is taking off, but the prospect of an emergency landing is looking increasingly inevitable. Both children missed their registration, and Hermione is currently sitting at her desk, organising her pencils furiously, ignoring the tears streaming down her face, sobbing and muttering to herself she hates Covid and school, and Mrs Plummer was nice, but maths was so BLOODY boring. Hermione has a little lisp lapse, and it's making her sound even more in need of a hug. Burt is in his room, also at his desk, silently letting big blobs of tears drop onto the page of his exercise book, staring into the abyss that is his life right now. He is on mute, and the video function is off. Unlike the other day, when he was not on mute, and I articulated some of my stronger feelings, like 'how many more fucking times do I have to say the same fucking thing to be fucking heard' as I walked out of Burt's room, in tears, to the stunned silence of Mrs Hickman and her class of twenty-something eight-year-olds being educated at a nice, centuries-old private school. That was fun. Burt came out then, face white as a sheet, which I thought was an interesting physiological reaction to stress, and said, "Mum, I wasn't on mute."

Now, in my kitchen, I am crying into my coffee, which is so strong it is probably going to give me a heart attack one of these days, hating myself for shouting at Burt again and furious with Don. I am blaming him. He would say for everything, but that's not true. I have myself to blame for that. Why am I experiencing the same disempowering, filled with dread and hopelessness, linked with the idea that his stuff is always more important than anything else. Why does the stuff he has to do trump everything? It is like the biggest ace card ever drawn.

'Because it pays the bills. Because it will allow us to pay off our mortgage and do whatever we want.' Don says, cross and loud. Later that afternoon, when the kids are upstairs, released and free from the tyranny of homeschooling, their mother is back once again to being a Mum or even Mummy, and definitely not Mrs How-Many-Times-Have-I-Told-You.

'Not everything in the world is about the bills.' I say feebly. This is not a good response. 'What about my business,' I try, 'that could pay some of the bills but now is dead in the water and just as it was taking off?'

'You can start again once we are out of this.' Don says, reasonably, he thinks.

'Seriously, Don, you have no idea about some things. Not everything business is business-related. My business is about people and the health of their minds. You can't just drop them when they are mid-self-harm and say sorry, buddy, we will pick this one up once this inconvenient global pandemic is over. In the meantime, hold that razor blade.' Obviously, I exaggerate here. None of my clients bring razor blades to their sessions, but the point has to be made.

'I told you to reschedule them to the afternoon, that's when I can be a bit more flexible, but I still might not be.' He gives with one hand and takes away with the other.

How this is supposed to be helpful, I wonder to myself for a thousandth time. He always does this by saying a thing followed by a contradiction, leaving you to make your peace with it. Or whatever you will.

'I can't just reschedule. This is not a one-off meeting; these people have, Don. This is a weekly, ongoing thing that they had to have awkward and difficult discussions about with their employers, or work around their partners' commitments or childcare when they are already struggling to get up in the morning.' I say, not exaggerating this time and thinking, not unlike me.

'Well, it can't be helped.' Don concludes as he walks towards his office, a cup of coffee in his hand. 'I have an important meeting. Make sure the kids are quiet.' He shuts the door, and I want to throw my cup at it, or him, and shout 'No.' And, 'Fuck you,' but I don't. The kids would hear, and Burt is already worried about the state of our marriage.

Instead, I shut the kitchen door, an act that enables the start of a peace process. Click, the kettle goes, and the sound of water slowly getting to the boil diffuses a little of the knot inside me. I breathe in, watching the steam from the kettle evaporate, and my mind returns to the client I saw earlier today. She was talking about her dad, who died recently.

Gwenda was fifty-six and very close to her dad. She was hit hard by her loss. Today, she recounted again going to see him in the hospital in his last days. She recalled, emotionally, how he told her to be a good girl and have a ten-minute cry, but no more. He wanted her to get on with her life after these ten minutes and not grieve for him. He was a gentle soul, Gwenda said with tears in her eyes. They used to play this game, she told me. Whenever she woke up, either from a nightmare or because it was the morning, she would knock on the wall that joined her room with her parents' room in a particular pattern, and he would respond.

This little ritual made Gwenda's world a happy, safe place. This reassurance he was there for her, on the other side of the wall. Now, he was on the other *other* side, and no matter how much she knocked, there was no reply. Suddenly, Gwenda felt very alone in the world. Her mum was still alive, but she couldn't close the gap on the loneliness that her father left behind him.

'I had a dream last night, which was very weird,' Gwenda had said in the session. People always think their dreams are weird. But if they unpicked them, one weird bit by the next, they would see the bits were just clues like you might get in an escape room game. The royal road to their deepest fears and desires. And, fears about desires being fulfilled.

'I was walking up some stairs, they were narrow and winding and really steep. There were no windows. It felt dark and quite scary. The only light coming in was from the very top. I don't know why, but I kept on going. It was some sort of a tower. As I was getting closer to the top, I was getting more scared, and then I saw my dad all the way up, telling me to come, and that everything would be ok.' Gwenda finished, apparently embarrassed by her dream. She was a hysterically private person, and I think I was the only human alive she had ever told things about herself that not even her dad knew. Things which she felt ashamed of, embarrassed by, guilty or worried about and things she felt scared of. Gwenda used to see a man in her room at night. He was not real, but she saw him as if he was. Most of the time, he would just sit in the chair in the corner of the room. Sometimes, he would be on the edge of her bed. She would only wake up her husband if it got too much, but most nights she could just go back to sleep. Maybe if there was an adjoining wall on which she could knock, the man might stop coming into her room. He started visiting shortly after her father died.

'Does the tower make you think of anything in particular? Do you feel you recognise it from somewhere?' I had asked Claire.

'I don't know, it all seems a bit silly now and I feel really childish talking about it.' Gwenda repeatedly tugged at her top as though it had risen up, trying to hide a part of herself. Her middle. She flicked the hair out of her face even though it wasn't in it.

'I wonder if you feeling childish tells us something about the dream. Perhaps it has some connection to your childhood?' I said.

'That's interesting. Now that you say that, I just remembered that Rapunzel was one of my favourite stories.' After a small pause, she added, 'and my dad used to joke about how many times he had to read it to me before I finally got over it.' Gwenda smiled, incredulous that the dream should not have been so silly after all.

'You did?'

'Well, I guess so. We all do, don't we? We have to.'

I wondered, though, if Gwenda ever got over it. In her dream, the one her mind produced, she was still stuck in the tower, a young girl, her dad her prince. Was this her fear, or was it her desire? To be held prisoner in her happy childhood.

After another pause, Gwenda added, 'And I now remember another thing in the dream. He was saying to me, come up, you can do this, Gwenda, you are a big girl now.' Gwenda had said, astonished.

'You are a big girl now.' I had repeated Gwenda's words.

She started crying then. 'It is as though he came back to see me in my dream. To tell me I was a big girl now and I could do this. I could be without him.'

Our conscious mind will only take from the dream what it can.

Was Gwenda stuck in the tower of her childhood, I ask myself as I fill my cup with boiling water. Her father's death, shaking up its foundations, she will need to grieve his loss as well as the loss of her childhood, which, through his living years, hasn't been possible for her to give up. I can't relate to this memory-experience that Gwenda has of her father. More than that, I find it uncomfortable. Like Goldilocks might have, I find my years-old seat suddenly either too big to too small, and no sign of the just right one. Thinking of my own position, I realise I too have been triggered. The little girl in me can't recognise any of the little girl Gwenda's feelings. It is incomprehensible to me. Like clapping with one hand. A stranger intruded into my consultation room, into our work, parading himself through this experience of Gwenda's of her father. The presence feels foreign in its softness, it sounds different with its gentle tone, it looks different, big but containing. I try to get through to the little girl inside me, speak to her in my adult voice, from my grown-up mind, but it is like I am knocking on the wrong door. Or, like, there is no one there to open it.

Looking around my own tower, walled off from the world by the invisible virus, I finish the last of my now lukewarm cup of tea and decide, with a sigh, to tuck into the third slice of chocolate cake that I bought in the local farm shop. The cake is exactly what a cake needs to be. I eat it slowly, and the cake, my hero, delivers. It makes everything better. Fortified by high amounts of sugar, I decide to take the children out for a walk to the nearby stream. We are so lucky to live in the countryside now. We can scream as much as we need to, and there are only sheep and pheasants to be alarmed by it. And we can go for lovely walks too, should such a thing be possible with a five and seven-year-old in tow.

'Kids?' I yell up the stairs, evenly, picnic packed and ready to go.

Nothing.

'Kids?' different intonation- but will it be enough?

Pause.

'Yes,' comes out of Hermione's room.

'Go and grab your bikes, we are taking a picnic to the stream.' I say.

'Yes!' comes out of Hermione's room this time, followed by hundreds of small elephants running across the upstairs landing, coming to a screechy halt at the stairs turn.

'Burt?' There is a threat in my voice now, 'Don't make me count to three.'

'Mummy.' Hermione says pitifully. 'That doesn't work with Burt. You always end up counting to five. At least. Sometimes ten, actually.'

'Do I?' I say, astonished that Hermione should notice this lapse, which is only one of many that I make daily when it comes to Consistency in Parenting.

'Yes, Mummy. Always.' Hermione's cute lisp makes me want to pick her up and cuddle her majestic squidgeness, ignoring the fact that I have just been picked up on parenting by a five-year-old.

'What do you think I should do?' I ask my five-year-old for some parenting advice, as I pick her up and give her a hug and kiss her lively cheeks as many times as she will let me get away with.

'I think we should leave without him, Mummy.' Earnest face as she says it, before adding, 'then he won't do it again.'

'Ok.' I put Hermione down, and we start walking towards the garage door to get the bikes. Despite my many flaws as a parent, I know some things Hermione doesn't, and one of them is that Burt has been listening to this conversation as he can't help but have a constant fear of missing out on something that Hermione gets to do.

'Coming!' A thousand bigger elephants are making the landing crossing this time.

We get onto the field behind our house, which will eventually take us to the stream hidden amongst tall trees, with the sun peering through a couple of openings, perfect for our picnic. The field is covered in green grass that's long because no one has been cutting it, and the kids get off their bikes to hide in it. As usual, I take an unnecessary amount of photos to capture the toothless smiles and funny faces, stopping to help Hermione, who is currently trying to put a dandelion in her hair. I could stare at their little faces forever, and looking at them up close, sitting in the grass fills my heart all the way to the top. Life can be good even in the middle of a hurricane if you find the right spot. I must have dozed off for a few seconds. It's been a long lockdown day.

'Muum.. Burt got in front of my bike and I fell.' Hermione is crying a little, but as I kiss her hurt finger, Hermione spots a hare darting across the field. Pulling her finger out of my hand, she shouts 'LOOK-A-BUNNY!', right into my unsuspecting ear. Fuck! I think that hurt.

'It's a hare,' says Burt, who knows his animals.

'I don't care, Burt. It looks like a bunny. I can call it bunny if I want, can't I, Mum?'

'Sure can.'

'But Mum, that's not right.' Burt insists. He cannot let things go.

'It is a hare, but she can call it a bunny because bunny is another word for a hare.'

'No. It's not. It's another word for a rabbit,' Burt says.

'Ok, Burtie. She is five. Why don't we let her get away with it?'

'I'm not a baby, Mum.' Hermione says with a quiver.

'I know you are not a baby, darling.'

'You are five, though.' Burt interrupts my attempt at reconciliation, condescendingly, 'which is closer to baby than seven.'

'Muum… Burt is being mean.' Hermione begins the complaints procedure and with it they are back in the hurricane and just before I feel myself losing the Judge and Jury position, a pheasant flies out of what feels like right underneath their feet and gives them a fright that makes them all scream out a different thing.

'Mummy, what is bastard?' Hermione asks.

Later that night, I get into my bed, beaten by the day. I had to put both children to bed tonight, and that always takes up most of my evening, and all that is left of my energy. My evening, I wonder if this is some blind belligerence on my part, to think of it as mine, the part of the evening that I, for some naïve reason, still think of as belonging to me. I am tired. I sigh, and as I do, I notice I have been sighing a lot lately. Sighing out loud is what I do when I am feeling stressed. Under pressure. The air pressure that has to come out. Making a big sighing song and dance about it. Sighing out loud makes me think of my mother. She used to sigh all the fucking time. And there it is. I spot it in my thoughts, hiding behind a little word. The anger. Always but a few steps behind the stress.

Having children is stressful. Having children when your husband is running a business in the city of London, with competitors on every corner, is stressful. Having children when you are trying to run your own business is stressful. Having children when your template for parenting is an angry man of unsound mind, and a weak woman driven by life to drink too much, is stressful.

But I wanted them. Once I was ready for them, or so I thought, *hah*, I wanted them so badly it hurt. The longing for a baby would squeeze the invisible yearning organ inside me, and it would grip so hard it could take my breath away. And I love them. I love them more than I have ever loved anything. More than I ever thought myself capable of loving. I would die for them. As I am lying in my bed, head heavy on the pillow, eyes heavier still, falling asleep is never difficult for me, a memory stalks in, light on its feet like a thief at night.

It's 2012. We are in our London flat, nestled amongst a few thousands of other London flats and offices, separated by the colonies of hooting, zigzagging cars, screaming ambulances, fire engines and an incessant hum of human chatter. Don and I are in our bedroom, four floors above the colonies, with triple-glazed windows which can't block out the sound of London life. We are in our very white, very new bed – king size, if you will. We have come a long way from our first bed, which we shared for one whole year at Christian's, and it didn't seem single at all. Lust works in mysterious ways. I am supported by an army of pillows, feeling ungainly as only a human with another human inside it will. The bedside lights are the good yellow that makes me feel calm, not like I am about to try and extract a whole human body, with head and everything. Recently, I had a dream in which I gave birth to my baby in body parts, separately. That was fun.

I am reading a book about pregnancy, which, I realise, too late, is mainly not the thing to do when you are actually pregnant. Should have read it before I had the half metre moving mass sticking out in front of me, attached to my abdomen. Don is next to me, with his laptop. Work is busy, and he takes it to bed with him. I put the book down and look at him.

'What shall we call him?' I ask.

'I don't know. Plenty of time yet to think about that,' he says, after a long pause. He is concentrating. He is not good at doing two things at the same time.

I know he doesn't want to talk. He doesn't want to talk right now, and he doesn't want to talk about *it*. But I do, so I say, 'I like thinking about it.'

'Sure. Write it down and we'll go through it nearer the time.' He says, voice even, but not lifting his eyes from the screen in front of him. Don doesn't get it. Or he does, but he has no time for it. I, on the other hand, I can't stop thinking about this baby inside me, and it gives me pleasure like no other to think about and talk about. Talking about it also makes it feel more real. Not that it isn't real, I can touch it and feel it, and I don't know why we humans have to put things in words to hear them or believe them, but I am incredulous that such an incredible thing could actually be happening to me. What with my humpty-dumpty past. But I don't push it because Don is frowning now. He is staring at his computer screen, frowning. The work is stressful. His business partner is being difficult, and Don fears there is a gorilla in his pack that is keen on coup d'etat. The second-in-command has a voice with that loudness one seems to unavoidably acquire at certain schools, at places hidden in the beauty of rural England, not hidden in their cost. Don's voice is deep and incisive and not manufactured by good education. It is his own, coming all the way from his gut, it is strong and it is free of the constraints of colonizing structures. I love Don's voice. A perfect baritone. A musical bar-in-tone.

'Don?'

'Yes?' Eyes fixed on the screen.

'I like your voice.'

'Eh?' he looks up.

I smile, and he closes his laptop. It's not always Rapunzel who has the singing voice, nor is it always the prince who has been blind before he found his love.

I am drifting off as I think about Don and his voice, and I smile in my mind. Yes, it was a terrible day, day 200 of Covid, but, no matter what, once the night falls and everything goes to sleep, we always meet in the middle, for better or for worse. His strong arms and the warmth of his body against my back, right here, in the middle of our king-size bed, here is my home. He is my home, I realise.

CHAPTER 6
I LEAVE PRAGUE IN SPRING

1996

Fourteen hours and forty-six minutes, you might not be counting

Seeing Leith at the coach station fills my stomach with the butterflies flipping about like they are on Ritalin. It's because Leith is at the coach station, and he is not supposed to be here. Veronika must have told him, her last attempt at changing my mind. This is annoying, and it is going to make my departure harder than it needs or ought to be. He is still indecently handsome. That slight frown and unrelenting gaze make him look like he is always a bit pissed off. Today, it's real and no less appealing.

It is a silent anger. Leith knows he has no rights left in this store. He didn't keep his receipt, and there are no returns available. He lost all rights over my body and the rest of me. The access he used to have was quite indiscriminate up until not that long ago. My generosity with myself has even earned me a toothbrush in his bathroom. But then, he overstepped the line. It is still too raw to think of it in a non-abstract way, to think of it for what it is. For what it was. To have a baby was not in the terms and conditions of our relationship. I had said quite clearly, "Strictly No Entry" to that particular crossing. There was no way I was ready.

He crossed unwittingly, sure. Sometimes, we wander into places in the excitement of the moment, thinking it will work out, we take the chance. But this was not his to take a chance with. He should have taken more care, I asked him to. This was not the sort of a thing you

54

take chances with. After, after everything was left unsaid and done, the most he could do was offer his opinion, reassurance, comfort, and promises. He could offer me some words. But I didn't want his words. And I didn't want to release him of his guilt. Not even in the slightest. I was angry, too.

Although completely silent, my anger manifests itself in ways that speak volumes. I am leaving. Not just Leith, but here, which includes any possibility of a repair of this broken thing. I am denying him forgiveness or understanding, all in dead silence.

I am angry because it was my body that had to bear the consequences of something the two of us brought around. I can see him heading to the stop where I need to catch her bus. He is giving me a space to say goodbye to Emile.

Emile says, 'What do you want to do?'

'Become invisible.' I am thinking fast, getting nowhere.

'I wonder why he is here.' Emile is not always helpful.

'To make me look him in the eye,' I say as I put my sunglasses on.

'Ah, well, you are good at that. Although it might be less satisfactory if you are invisible. For him, at least.'

'Emile. I don't want to look him in the eye. He is like the male version of Scheherazade, and he hasn't yet had his one thousand and one nights.'

Emile looks confused. 'But she was telling the stories so that he wouldn't kill her, no?'

'Yes, Emile. And even though I am not contemplating killing him, I am definitely trying to kill him off in my mind, do you see? That is why I am leaving. No more stories. Kill him off because I killed something else we made together. Because I am not ready to make things together. And he is not the person I want to be making things with. And, I am not a person he wants that sort of a thing with either.'

I almost patiently explain this to Emile while listening to my own voice to see if I can convince myself of the truth of what it's saying.

'Doesn't look like that from where I am standing.' Emile says while he is not standing at all but walking, watching Leith as he starts walking towards them.

'Things almost never are what they seem to be, Emile.' Turning to him, I extend my hand to take the bag he carried for me and embrace him with my free arm, planting a kiss on his cheeks three times for luck. 'Thank you, Emile. Come and see me soon, ok?'

'You will be back.' More of a question than a statement. He is sad. I can tell, and so am I but there is Leith now, stopped a few steps back. People are respectful of goodbyes in a way they are not respectful of almost any other social encounter. It is a curious thing. People step away from sadness when given a chance. Look away, or look but not be seen looking.

'Bye, Emile, don't be too good while I'm gone, ok?' I say to his back, and he raises his arm and gives a little salute as he walks off into the cobbled streets of this ancient city that holds so many of my footsteps.

'You didn't tell me.'

No, hello, no, how are you? Leith has no time for small talk now.

'No.' I don't know if he means about the 'unfortunate incident' or my leaving. He looks so good. He is standing too close. I can smell his aftershave, and I can see the soft lines on his neck and around his eyes. His eyes are boring into me like fire irons, stirring up a right flame in the pit of my gut. I need an extinguisher. I look around as though there could possibly be one lying around somewhere. The bus arrives, and people start loading their luggage into the belly of the coach, soon to be crammed like boxes underneath a rich person's Christmas tree.

'And now you are leaving.' Leith continues with no attempt at linking the sentences with any unnecessary linguistic ornaments.

'Yes.' I can play that game.

'You are angry with me, and this is my punishment.' He concludes his indictment list.

Fairly accurate, I think but don't say, and I look away because it is suddenly way too hot for March.

'When are you going to grow up, M?' Now the prosecution begins.

'In what way?' My eyes back on him now, in focus, ablaze with their own hazardous materials.

'When are you going to stop running?' he says, and I don't understand how he can look at me so intently without looking away once. Doesn't he feel the heat?

'I am not running. I am leaving.' I say, totally unconvincingly, suddenly aware of the sweat on my back as though I just sprinted the whole way.

'At some speed.' He knows. He knows what I look like when I'm sweating hot.

'Not really. I was walking the whole time, didn't you see? I just have no reason to delay.'

It's feeble but it will have to do. Not long now.

'Really? Is what we had, what we have,' he corrects himself, 'not a reason to delay? Pause, at least? Think it over? Talk to me? Make me a part of this conversation you had with yourself about us? It wasn't just your thing, M. It was our thing. I…' there is a pause that feels like it weighs a ton, and he is fighting his face to not betray him.

'What?' he will never say it. He will never say it because it is not true.

'I care about you.' Still looking and searching for something in my face. It must be something really small because he is looking so intently that it feels like he will burn a hole into my soul with his eyes.

I decide to look back at him now, matching the weight of the pause with my eyes.

'The problem is, Leith, I don't believe you.' I don't say I want to. I also don't say that even if I did want to, I can't. It is beyond me to believe that he cares about me. He, or that anyone could, for that matter. A long way beyond. We just had great sex and a good conversation, and that was quite hard to leave behind. But it would never work. We could never work. I could not see it working. We are too similar. Two fireplaces. You don't have two fireplaces in one room. It would be an overkill. Too hot. And it would eventually burn the whole house down. I look away. He stays silent, defeated.

'I think you are right. I think I need to grow up or something. I need to grow for sure. For one, see my feet? They are tiny, and they have no roots. I have these feet with no roots, and so I am going to go now and walk up to that bus, up those stairs, and I'll sit by that window over there, and I won't look back at you because it will make me really sad. I will miss you, Leith.' I say, looking at him again, swallowing the sadness building up at the back of my throat. What a stupid place for sadness to build a sand castle.

'Don't do this, M.' He moves towards me, and I take a step back like a red-light-green-light game.

'You don't'. I whisper as he moves forward again, pulls me in and holds me until I stop resisting it and rest my body weight on him. 'Thank you,' I say to his shoulder, 'for everything. It was special, and I don't know why it had to end, but it did. That thing that happened ended it for me. I can't get past that.'

He holds me for a bit longer, breathing me in, and now I am conscious of my hot sweat. He doesn't say anything else and then he takes my hand and my bag and takes it into the bus, holding my hand as he passes the bag to the red-faced coach driver. And then he has to let go.

I did look out of the window. He stood there and waited until the coach disappeared around the corner and suddenly, just like that, with one turn of a bus, I was all alone in the world again.

CHAPTER 7
HOW THINGS ARE NOT JUST WHAT THEY SEEM TO BE

LONDON, 2014

Supervision is many things, but what it is not is Super Vision.

I am in my little car. It's an old, A-class Mercedez, and I love it. I kick the hell out of its gear stick, and Don is not too happy about it. I am not doing it on purpose, I just don't know any other way of driving. Or living. I am making a call hands-free but there is nothing else that feels free about me right now. No better than a spooked horse, my emotions have overtaken my capacity to think. I decide to pull over to try to rein them in. Tears are not listening; they are streaming down my face against my will and dropping with attitude into my cup of coffee like kids jumping into muddy puddles. The coffee is black and too hot. The heat of the dark bitter drink is not contained by the plastic cup, which is burning my hand, forcing me to grunt "fuck" as I hold it in the same hand for too long. I swap hands while waiting for Claudia to pick up her phone. My eye catches the glint of my Grandma's wedding ring on my finger. The ring has a heart on it made of rose gold and it sits embedded on three lines of thin gold. Thin gold, like thin ice grandma skated on all her life. Not that she even complained. Only to God.

Interrupting a trip down memory lane, Claudia's voice floats out of the car speakers with some presence. Like the genie in a bottle, I know she will do her magic. Claudia is also in training, but she is two years my senior. She treats me like I might conceivably know more than she does, which is not true. I am beginning to suspect that treating people like they know more than her is how Claudia approaches life in general. Which, on the face of it, seems very mature, but, in Claudia's case, it may also be something else. Psychoanalysts call it "symptomatic". It might just hide a few unresolved events, and it is also a sophisticated act of passive aggression. Claudia was a nurse in her previous career. Her husband was a surgeon. He still is. Claudia has Italian parents, and you can tell this by looking at her. She is petite, curvy and beautiful. She has an elongated nose that gives her an air of knowing and restrained thick, dark hair, which imbues the knowing with magic. "Hello?"

I introduce the topic as if we are continuing an old conversation, which, to some extent, we are, 'I hate him, Claudia.'

'Oh dear. What happened?' Claudia floats through the dashboard speakers, trying to anchor the story.

'I don't know, exactly,' I say, because I don't. 'We had an extra supervision session, which he had offered because of that tricky client.' One of my clients works for the government in a department which, despite having a very dramatic-sounding name, literally just spells out what it is. An ordinary, uniquely unimaginative, plain old acronym. I have wondered if being uniquely unimaginative was a pre-requisite for the employees' personalities too, until I started to unpeel this onion. But it's much worse than that.

'We had the meeting in his house, which was kind of weird in itself as we usually have it in a group, as you know,' I blow my nose before continuing, 'and I told him the summary of the session, going into more detail over the difficult bit.' I pause before adding, 'You know when he does that annoying teacher-like peering through the top of his glasses look?' I look at myself in the car mirror as I'm saying this, imitating the look, red-eyed, mascara putting on a watercolour performance underneath my eyes.

'Yes,' Claudia says, adding, 'I don't think he is consciously patronising or angsty. Or, at all…' which I ignore, for now, and carry on. 'He then says he noticed I didn't have any notes to hand.' I pause to blow my nose again, closing the mirror flap with resignation. Sometimes, all you can do with blackness is to smudge it.

'Did you have them with you?' Claudia asks matter-of-factly.

'No, Claudia, I did not.' I say, a wobble in my tone.

'I am just thinking it probably means something,' Claudia says, 'you know if you didn't this time but you normally do…'

'Yes, maybe. I kept having these weird images during the session. At one point, I found myself wondering if she had a knife in her handbag. Which was unusual. Anyway, I said I didn't have them because I left them at home, which wasn't true, I didn't get to write any. I have no idea why I lied. Like a kid caught doing something wrong!' I say, getting caught up on a side track in my mind about the borderline definition. It troubles me. The border is meant to be between psychosis and neurosis, but I could see no border, however symbolic. All I could see was a movement on a spectrum. I force my mind to return to what Claudia is saying.

'Did you catch your client doing something wrong?'

I know Claudia is referring to a phenomenon that happens in supervision sometimes, when the thing that happens between the client and the therapist in a session is re-enacted in some way in supervision, between the supervisor and the supervisee.

'Not exactly, but I felt uncomfortable, almost unsafe. Which was weird.' I say and start wondering if my supervisor felt unsafe about me being in his house. I did take a very long time in the toilet. I held that pee for the whole morning. 'Be that as it may, I couldn't think about this with him. He was being too persecutory, and in the end, I said he was aggressive, and I felt uncomfortable. He said he was just being assertive, and I said I was sorry, but I didn't agree. Which I wasn't, by the way.'

'You weren't what, sorry? Claudia is obviously confused. I am probably rambling.

'I wasn't sorry, Claudia. That's what I wasn't. I wasn't sorry one tiny bit. And he was furious. He said he offered me this extra session. Did I remember, he didn't have to do that. And, I turn up, no notes and not happy with what he has to say. I said it was how he was saying it, whether he called it aggressive or not, I couldn't actually hear him because of it. And what has it got to do with anything that I had no notes? Where are we? At school? Let us recall for a moment, I am doing this for free.' I keep on and I know Claudia is not clear now if I have said all of this to the supervisor or am just saying it now. The latter would be preferable. But I press on.

'I said I didn't understand why he was pointing out he offered me this extra session. Was he asking me to be grateful, Claudia? For doing his job for which he gets paid, or should my inferior role in this relationship auto-include masochistic tendencies? Should I derive pleasure from being bullied? What is it with people, Claudia? Why do people always have to be thanked?'

'Oh dear,' Claudia says. 'That didn't go well, did it.'

'No.' I sniff and start to compose myself. 'It didn't.' Un-composing myself for just one more thing, I say, 'He IS a bully, you know. Hiding under a supervisor's cloak.'

'Oh dear.' Claudia says again.

I begin to wonder if Claudia's sense of propriety, which is strong, will let her say anything other than oh dear. I watch as cars pass by on the road, some drivers looking quizzically in my direction, others steadfastly away lest I try to flag them down for help. I notice my hands in my lap, squeezing the life out of the tissue paper already half destroyed by my tears. Still angry, then.

'I am sure it's not as bad as it feels,' she says eventually.

'Claudia. If it feels bad, it is bad because that is what it feels. Bad.'

'Yes, but it will pass.'

'You want to bet?' and then, recalling my more mature part and remembering Claudia is not the enemy, I concede a small point. 'In a couple of years, maybe. It will transition from rage to intermittent indignation. But I would actually bet you my bottom dollar, it will still have the capacity to trigger me in my old age.'

Claudia laughs, and then I laugh because the thought is suddenly funny. What isn't funny at all is that I need this man to write me an assessment for my end-of-the-year review, and I'm fucked if I'm going to apologise to him. 'Before you say it,' I say to Claudia, 'I have nothing to apologise for as far as I am concerned.' I know there is an edge to my voice. To apologise would be to sell my soul to the devil himself. Because I wouldn't mean it, and I don't say things I don't mean. Ever. For better or worse.

'Oh dear.' Claudia says again, but this time in the way you might filet a fish using a really sharp knife.

'No.' I say like you might choke on its bone.

'Sleep on it, M. You must have tapped into something. You both ended up reacting to something other than each other. You know this, right?'

'Well, he should not be a supervisor then.'

I know I sound harsh. I sound harsh even to me, but harsh meets harsh; that's how it goes with me.

'Maybe. But maybe it is a very useful thing that happened between you.'

'I hate when someone is trying to force something on me, Claudia.'

'I know, M, I know you do.'

'Like it is ok to force a thought on someone,' I continue, explaining myself to her because I don't want Claudia to think I am as harsh as I am, 'because he is in a position of some authority over me. I mean, I hate recipes, Claudia.'

'Well, he is.'

'What? A recipe for disaster?'

'In a position of authority,' Claudia says, bracing herself before adding, 'to you.'

Also bracing myself because I like my colleague, I say that he has more experience, yes, which in theory should make him more able to relate to people. Adding a less pointed, 'Right?'

'Well…' Claudia tries, but I haven't finished yet.

'But he isn't, is he. He is not able to relate to people as he should. He is not using his power wisely. He is not sharing it either, his wisdom. He is forcing it. He is forcing his experience, or if you like, authority, which is to say himself, on me. Not cool. If you try to force yourself on someone with your ideas or ways of thinking, it is like a thought rape, and you are going to come up against some resistance. A lot of resistance in my case. Force creates force. If you are pushed, you tense up to stop yourself from falling backwards. You tense up even if you decide not to push back. So yeah. He needs to unbully himself.'

'But there is a possibility, M, that it is about how *you* hear him, right? That the didactic look to you is a fatherly look to me. That angst is another side of kindness. That his opinion isn't forcing itself on me, rather it is guiding me.'

'Yes.' I say because she is right, it is possible.

'And, I am sure when he reflects on this, he will have something to say about it. Give it a week until the next group supervision and reassess then.'

'I will.' I say. I might not agree with what she is saying, but I feel better about speaking to her. Claudia has a voice that has a care in it; it is like a tiny dose of opiate, or rather its legitimate version, because Claudia is an above-the-board kind of a person, with that voice that makes acute things recede into the background and take on a gentler tone. She holds me over the phone line, and when I say, 'Thank you, Claudia, you are the best,' I mean it.

'He is not that bad either, M. Something just cross-wired today. He has a high opinion of you, too.'

I don't believe her, but I won't say it. Instead, I make a joke that's not funny, and I say, 'High, is it?' I am laughing. Some things you laugh off, some you kick into shape, but they are means to the same end. 'That is precisely his problem. He needs to come down from his fine-looking high horse and see the difference in the perspective.' Even though I am laughing, I notice something else creeping in, the vocal fry betraying me to myself. The scratchy sound that says *Claudia is being an apologist, you know that, don't you?* And hearing the reply in my head, I heard all too many times before *we are not all like you, Meli* as if that was a good enough reply to the problem that is patriarchy. We are two women using different strategies to cope with it. Strategies based on our own relationships with our fathers.

When you are standing in a picture that is being taken, you don't see things which you will see when you look at the picture later. Driving away from the roadside, I now see with a clarity which you don't get when you are too close to a thing. The supervisor incident was about my father. It felt too much to be in the room alone with him. It felt as if he was trying to scare me, using his authority over me like a virtual cane to make me comply with his chain of thoughts, gaslighting me, gaslighting himself. Holding the knife to my ribs for no good reason. Just because he could and just because I couldn't do anything about it. That was the only way I could hear him at this point in my life. Whether or not he was a bully.

But I need to drive now. I need to go and be a mother.

Being a mother is one of the problems you come up against when you change your policy of being a girl with no roots.

As I drive home, Lenny Kravitz and his Fly Away playing on the radio parachutes me into the summer of 1998. I was in east London then, single and reckless, with no one telling me what to do or expecting me to thank them for it. In this scene from over a decade ago, a phone rings. It's an old-fashioned phone with an old-fashioned ring. The phone is black and clunky, hanging on the wall in a hallway with chipped plaster walls. The hallway is the centre of the roundabout that makes up this house, so you can hear the phone ringing in every part of it. My room is upstairs. I am an au pair. Cathy and Geordie, my employers, are in the kitchen. They will be there first. Anyway, I wouldn't try to answer the phone. It's theirs, not mine. I have no such ties to the world just yet.

Also, there is no one really to call me at this number. I haven't been here very long.

'M?' comes a yell from downstairs, in Geordie's unmistakably impenetrable north-of-England accent. 'There is a call for you.'

'Erm, ok, thank you.' I yell back, coming down the stairs, thinking how weird.

'Hello?' It's a question.

'Hi, M, it's Don.' Don says, expectant of something.

'Oh. Hi!'

'Hi, you sound surprised.' Don says, less expectant now but cheerful nonetheless.

'Oh, I just didn't think I gave you my new number.'

'Well, it was late, and we'd had a few,' he says, laughing.

'Yes, we did.' I say, thinking how much I like the sound of his voice.

'Although, there is a funny story.' Don continues.

'Oh yes?' Uh oh.

'Yes. I had to try five times before I got you.'

'Why is that?' I ask, wondering how many people would speak to four different people and try again. Just to try to reach me. Also, I like the idea of him getting me. It sounds like a good game. He won't have to try five times.

'I couldn't work out your handwriting.'

That was the moment I fell in love with Don for the first time.

Pulling into their driveway nearly twenty years later, I park next to Don's reliable old estate car. Don is the only man I ever met who could stand up to my father. The only man I ever knew who could withstand my father's troubled legacy. And he did it using one thing only. Kindness. Over and again. Like a tree which no wind can disturb.

CHAPTER 8
PRAGUE, 1996

THE LAST CHRISTMAS I GAVE HIM MY HEART

And Some Unfinished Business

It's Christmas, and I am back on the cobblestoned streets. How I love the clip-clop of the heels on the stone. It's freezing cold in Prague in a way it never is in England. The cold penetrates my bones as if I am wearing nothing, not even my skin, even though I am wrapped snug as a bug in a worn sheepskin jacket I got in the second-hand shop in London. Second-hand sheepskin will do me just fine. I am not good at looking after things, and red wine always wants to get spilt when in my hands. And things should be used, enjoyed, not worried about. If you shop in a second-hand shop, it is of little consequence. If you live your life like it is a second-hand life, what is the consequence?

I find a phonebooth and get out my change to call Veronika. We are due to meet today. Lifting the phone receiver off the hook, I look at the stickers that cover the booth making all kinds of promises, your call. The phone receiver holds the smell of other people's breath; it is warm despite the outside temperature, and I imagine that it retains a memory of words passed into it. If only it could talk. Payphones are like hungry dogs, too. There never seems to be a satisfying ratio between the rate at which the coins are consumed to what needs to be said. It makes me think of Father. His shortness whenever I called, which really wasn't often, was sparse as though telephones were telegraphs. Waste no words. Words equalled coins in his mind. He probably could see the coins feeding the call, disappearing before his eyes.

'Hi!' Veronika says. 'The next tram is in ten minutes, so let me dash! See you soon! Oh my God, I can't believe you are here!'

'See you in Jo's.' I say, smiling into the receiver, which responds with 'byeeeeee', and the sound of the line cuts off.

I put the receiver back on its hook and step out of the booth. The door of the booth is hanging, not quite closed behind me, and I am back in freezing Prague. As I start walking, it occurs to me that Glen might be at Jo's, too. Glen is one of my ex-boyfriends and he happens to own the pub where I am meeting my old friends. Glen is a good guy so we were never going to work out. I slept with his best friend by accident when Glen went home to visit his mum in Canada. It was all a bit unfortunate. Veronika probably told him I was coming. She was good like that, Veronika, always challenging my perception of where I stood on things. Walking through the Charles Bridge, I smile as I pass a group taking turns with their hands on the stone that grants good fortune.

It has been four months since I left. It feels good being back. Everything is soothingly familiar; the smell of freedom lingers. I am enjoying the crisp taste of the cold air, the snowy blanket on the streets and the towers of the Castle. The snow trespassing on people's hats and scarves and it makes them smile, the warm air coming out of their mouths as they speak to each other. Christmas is in the air. And with it, this expectation that even Ebenezer Scrooge got sucked into, that Christmas will deliver magic for all. I know, it's a little Peter Pan, that eternally child-part of the human make-up, living on in us for eternity. We all, even the most unlikely, let ourselves hope for a miracle in this Neverland that is Christmas. We all believe, for this fraction of the year, in the unbelievable. The hypnotic hysteria of Christmas time is powerful.

Not everyone, I reprimand myself. Not everyone will believe that. You have to have some hope left in order to believe. I wonder how deep human hope is. It is not a bottomless well. Still, everything looks so pretty at Christmas. It *looks* hopeful. Maybe because it all looks so hopeful, it feels hopeful, too. The snow covers up all the imperfections, a white illusion of peace, and people are happy to forget for the moment that it will melt soon enough. I am totally prepared to forget it for today, too. Soaked in the magic of the atmosphere, I feel embraced by a warm glow dancing in defiance of the tiny icicles hanging off my hat. I feel nice. It is just a moment in time, I know. It will pass, illusion replaced by disillusion or some kind of reality, but this is a good moment and I am going to paddle in it for a while. It is that moment, or a fragment of one, which makes me keep at it, keep at life. You need lots of them, millions, really, tiny fragments of moments like this, which, if you are lucky, will add up enough to balance the necessary misery and drudgery that come with life. You have to collect these moments, feel them in your hands, admire them, taste them, cry them, play with them. And then put them away somewhere safe. These tiny moments of warm glow under your skin, where snow is covering up messy things. The memory will come in handy one day.

And here I am. I have arrived at the bar door. There is a thick, black curtain covering the windows all the way to the floor. It keeps the cold out. Most bars have it; it's a nod to the winter freeze. An extra layer to the sixties builds, harnessing the warmth and leaving the cold at the door with a strange in-between space. A space to transition between the elements on either side, depending on which direction you are going. Get ready to be cold. Get ready to get hot. How hot? I stop here to take a deep breath, and with it, the familiar smell that comes from a room full of people and cigarette smoke and spilt beer and wine. It is a bodily atmosphere in which memories come, flash up and go on a never-ending reel. Enter Me.

I see them straight away. They are in their usual spot, in the corner, up a few steps, next to the fireplace. It exudes heat and the right colour, which suits all complexions and souls indiscriminately. They are talking to each other, animated, alive with their stories of the day. Watching them from this distance before they can see me feels strange. They are the same people, in the same spot, doing the same thing. Without me.

It's as if no time has passed. They are all there. Veronika, Beth, Svetlana, Emile and Ray. The core of my Prague Matrix, without me. A casual reminder of my impermanence. Veronika sees me first, and she stands up with the heavy chair, making a banshee out of the stone floor. Then they all turn, and Ray shouts out, "Here she is, de English-voman!" and there are hugs and kisses and space made for me. I can't help it; it feels weird, but I just need a drink to make that go away. When the conversation finally settles down into smaller groups and smaller weirdness, Veronika leans into me and says, 'I bumped into Leith…' Lighting her cigarette and holding the light for me.

'Hope it didn't hurt.' I say I am annoyed. I specifically asked Veronika not to bump into Leith.

'He said he will be at Café Rouge later. If you fancied it.'

'Fancied "it"?' dragging on my cigarette, I briefly estimate how much I fancy the idea of Leith waiting for me in Café Rouge. A deep pull in the pit of my stomach answers me convincingly.

'Well, I didn't want you to miss out on anything, Ms.' Veronika grins. She means on any dilemma. She loves presenting me with dilemmas, especially ones which might lead me back to Prague.

'No, I bet. You are that kind of a friend.' I say, reluctantly returning the grin.

'How has it been?' Veronika asks like she is stepping on someone's toes.

'Peaceful.' It's true that spending time inside the circle of a family who can afford to pay for childcare goes a long way to being peaceful. At least to begin with. Before peace metamorphoses into ennui. It is a necessary order of things, I think. If people didn't get bored with the state of things, people would never end up doing anything. Thus, you could say that boredom leads to progress. I smile as I'm thinking this, about to share it with Veronika who could be reading my mind.

'Sounds boring.'

'Well, I can speak English now. Especially all the words to Tracey Chapman songs.'

'When are you coming back?' Veronika asks, not impressed with The Fast Car that I have got myself.

'Things are still new, you know, lots to explore, language to learn. So not yet.' I say, adding, 'What about you?' We wrote to each other, so I know there is a new man in Veronika's life. He owns a flower business. She has been working for him for a while, and naturally, being a good-looking man, Veronika has decided to have a play.

'He is married,' she replies, 'which was ok to begin with.'

'Did his wife say so?' I ask, adding, 'What changed?'

'She is pregnant.' Veronika says, ignoring the bait.

'Oh shit, Niks. He's been having his cake and eating it.' But I am aware of a sudden tight squeeze in my abdomen, where once were forty-six chromosomes holding on for dear life. Once, not that long ago.

'Yes. Not cool. None of it feels very cool anymore.' Veronika says, pulling hard on her cigarette.

'Call it?' I mean a day. Call it a day.

'He reckons he is going to leave her,' pausing for a second, 'for me.'

'Ah. And what do you reckon?' I feel a bit numb. It is as though I have called on one of my inner layers to speak for me. I don't like this thing making noises inside me, a thing that feels increasingly like what people call a "moral stance".

'Well, he is forty-two.' Veronika exhales the smoke of her Camel light straight into my face.

'What does that mean?' ignoring the smoke challenge. It is trying to unbalance the "moral stance", she knows.

'He should know.'

'He should know what?'

'Better. He should know better.'

'Better than what? Better than who?' the Stance still standing.

'I don't know, M. Are you judging me?' Veronika asks incredulously.

'No. Maybe. I don't think so, though.' I reply honestly, 'Are you?'

'Of course.' Veronika finishes the last of her drink, putting out the cigarette that has started to burn her fingers now.

'Let's have another drink,' I say. I don't want to know anymore. I don't want to know what Veronika is going to do with this. It is going to happen whether or not I have an opinion on it. Whether or not I have a moral stance on it. And I will it to go away.

Emile comes over and gives me a side hug, 'I missed you.' We all walk to the bar together to get another round of drinks. The music is on, and Glen has a new girlfriend. She looks a bit like me.

The evening goes predictably enough. Like we always used to, we philosophise about things that will never change the world, or only if we could first change ourselves, and we laugh at our incompetence at growing up or growing rational, and we drink, drink too much, blowing smoke in each other's faces to touch something without hurting it. Nothing much has changed, and yet everything feels like I have come into the wrong country by accident. How is that possible, I wonder. Later, we sing and dance so that we don't have to think about how lonely we feel in the world because when you are drunk, you might be numb in some places, but you feel other ones all too clearly. And then, Jo's is closing and the only place within walking distance open at this hour is Café Rouge. And I can't resist this walk. There is something there, at the end of it, that needs to be finalised. And I don't care what my moral Stance makes of it.

Back at Leith's, our reunion is stronger than the wind was in our faces on the way there, it is more than a smoke without a fire. A consequence of something still smouldering, embers of desire not yet extinguished. I am in his bed, at once familiar and not, has he had another woman in there since I left? Probably. His arms under and over me, he tells my back he can't get me out of his head. I am always there. Day and night. How cool, I think, I can be in two countries at once, but I don't say that it doesn't seem like the right moment. I come into his dreams like a tease, which makes waking up a daily nightmare. He misses me. He didn't realise how much of him I would take with me when I left. Can he have it back? Hopefully, they are not all nightmares, which is another thing I don't say.

I am slow to roll over, to face his dark, chiselled face, a dear face, a face I am very fond of. I touch it with my fingers as if to feel all the different things I can see in there and things reflecting from my own. But doubt is all I can see in the end. And that won't do. I take my hand back under my chin and say quietly, sorry, I don't have it. So he quietly takes what I have, what I will let him have. Both of us know we have arrived at the moment when a movie is about to come to an end. But we make the ending outdrawn. After, he lights us a cigarette and lies back with his head propped up by his arm, a frown creasing his handsome face. We breathe our sweat and silence because all is said and done now because all things must come to an end.

Quietly, as if trying not to break something, he says, 'This is not a movie, you know, M? This thing you live, it is not a movie, you are not a character in a play or a sole director of it. You have to start living like this is real. Because it is the only real we can know. And one day, you will wake up and realise it, and it will be late.'

'Late for what?' *Wake up!* The menacing words of my father sneak in to make things more unbearable still.

'I don't know.' He says, suddenly defeated by my tone and he walks away to get dressed. He means for us. It will be too late for us.

'Can I stay the night?' I ask, trying to go back to the moment when we were not thinking about the future. When we were solely being just here and now, when everything was just fine. But I know I'm clutching onto a broken straw.

'Sure. Always.' Pulling his jumper over his head, he says, 'I'll go and stay in the office.'

I don't try to change his mind. I don't even ask why because I know. It hurts. It hurts me, too. I don't know why I can't just stay or come back and be with Leith and be normal. He seems to really care about me, and he is clever and funny and we have an amazing time when it comes to forgetting who we are. I just know that I can't.

And so Leith leaves his flat, leaves me in his flat, which used to feel like it had two fireplaces, but now it's arctic, and he goes and sleeps alone in his office. He doesn't hug me to say goodbye. He just leaves and closes the door after himself. I already know what to do with the key. In the morning, I decide I would leave Prague earlier than I planned. There is no point in staying. Something tells me this is over. Not just Leith. This part of my life is over. No more bed-floating. Dorothy has arrived. She arrived somewhere. Even if she doesn't know where, what it is or what the future holds, she is on the Yellow Brick Road.

The following day, waiting for the bus at the coach station again, I feel like a heroine in a French film's *Deja Vu* and I think I need to start living like it's real.

CHAPTER 9
ALL THE FUN YOU CAN HAVE IN EAST LONDON

1997

Loose, Luze, Lost.

Fourteen hours and forty six minutes is the quickest you can get to London from Prague on a coach. It is 1,271km of time you have to think about things you are leaving behind. Germany, the Netherlands, Belgium, France, and finally, England. We go through the Dartford Crossing into London and take the M25 towards Bexleyheath, Docklands, Canary Wharf, Wapping, Tower Hill, and Victoria Coach Station.

From one coach station to another. Is it out of the frying pan into the fire? I guess I will just have to find out. Ready or not.

Your past comes back and hooks you. You are a fish, dangling at the end of the line that someone else is reeling in. Back and forth, back and forth. Your past is the puppet master. In Māori you say ka mua ka muri. You have to look back in order to move forward. The future comes up from behind. Sigmund Freud founded a whole new science when he said, "Where id is, there shall ego be". We must turn unconscious into conscious if we are to stand a chance of being let off that hook. Carl Jung warned of the dangers of the collective shadow, the unknown side of our societies' selves, and urged us to get to know it lest we fall prey to its pull. The message seems clear enough. Acquaint yourself with your unconscious thoughts and become in charge of your story. But how do you find out about the things in your head you don't know are there?

You find it in your dreams, and you find it in the slips of the tongue and in the things you do, over and again, things which don't make sense and don't make you happy, yet you keep on doing them. You replace an act with a thought. So that's how you unhook yourself from the Lady Past. Of course, for a long time, you might have liked the Lady and her straitjacket. But you won't forever.

Paul is Angela's rather ineffective husband. Angela is a PE teacher at a local primary school, and Paul is an actor. They have two kids with French names, God knows why, and the only acting I have ever seen Paul do was at home, where he regularly threw tantrums more accomplished than those of his three-year-old who was not as "good as gold", as they like to tell their friends. I am currently Paul and Angela's au pair, and I never see Paul go to work, which is more than a bit annoying as he really appears good for nothing. What use is being "on par" with a man-child who specialises at being good for nothing, I wonder as I clear up the kitchen after the breakfast tsunami that only one and three-year-old children can muster.

Paul is hovering, making a cup of tea, and then he says, to me, I think, 'She is a bit loose.' Earlier, he and Angela were talking about a woman I recently met at one of their parties, which they seem to throw in order to tell themselves everything is ok. Paul probably thinks he is very cool telling his young au pair that a friend of his is "a bit loose." He sounds conspiratorial and gossipy. Like a woman, they say, but he is a man. My English is not quite up to date yet with the many ways in which women can be branded in this language, although daily I see words like "loose" burned into the skins of their souls, scars unveiled by too thick make-up and lips made to look swollen. It's not hard to guess Paul is being nasty about the woman.

'Loose?' I say, 'like she got lost? Has she gone missing?'

'No, no,' Paul laughs, condescending as fuck, 'loose like she sleeps with a lot of men.'

'Oh,' I say. 'I sleep with a lot of men. Does it mean I am "LUSE"?' I deliberately mispronounce the word.

Paul goes red and says, 'No, no, not like that."

'Oh. Not like that. Like what?' I say, enjoying his discomfort. What a prick. I heard he likes to dress up. I wonder if there is a shaming name for it.

Later, when I am upstairs, in my little au-pair room, I look up the word. Promiscuous, uninhibited, unrestrained, philandering. Licentious and loose. It might as well say "only pertaining to women" and probably does, somewhere. No man in the history of the world has been given the adjective, loosely and without any inhibition whatever, to describe his sexual escapades. In his case, they are only manifestations of his manly prowess. Despite this, no, in fact, because of this, I flaunt my very personal disinhibition like it is a trophy.

My new friend Jane, on the other hand, also an au pair, is the very opposite of disinhibited. She is so inhibited that the word is not sufficient to describe the gaping abyss where her capacity for abandonment slept. Jane has become a member of her au-pair family in a more traditional way than me. She is busy sleeping with the man of the house. In the absence of a permanent housewife, she also loves his children a bit too much for my liking or understanding. It seems like an exciting arrangement except for the children's bit. What if the kids walked in on them? Poor kids. What were they supposed to make of it? Daddy, why is Jane in your bed? Is she our new mummy now? Anyway, Jane isn't like me. This means she is not in it for fun. She is in it because she wants to marry Manjit. Which is obviously not going to happen. As is usual in these cases, it is obvious to everyone except Jane.

Later on, in Manjit's house, I am retelling Jane my little *tete-a-tete* with Paul. Jane is laughing while also shaking her head. 'M, you shouldn't tell people you sleep with a lot of men.' Not condescending, not judging. Jane understands that girls need to have fun and it's her only hope of experiencing it, to live it vicariously through friends like me, and she loves me for it. This has happened to me before. I seem to enable women. For better or worse, some might argue. 'Anyway, that should teach him, silly prick.' Jane says. 'A little prick, non?' I say with what I think is a French accent, and we laugh. I am sitting in Manjit's bathtub on a small step that kids use to reach the sink to brush their teeth. I am wearing my pants and bra and Jane is applying the hair colour into my outgrown roots. We have become close because that can happen when you are a young girl in a foreign country. There is an easy camaraderie between us and some oblique sense of safety. You need this kind of thing if you have no roots.

We are going out tonight, and I am excited. Something exciting happens most nights we go out, in this little borough of the great city of London. Jane is fed up with Manjit. He keeps promising her he is going to tell the children the truth about their relationship, but each deadline she gives passes, and even Jane is beginning to wonder if the deadline is actually dead.

'I think he might be using me,' she says. I am glad my head is down, and Jane can't see my face. I am not good at hiding my thoughts, but I don't want to hurt Jane's feelings. They are already quite battered.

So instead, I tentatively say, 'Well, at least you are having some fun in the meantime, right?'

'Oh God, not really,' Jane exhales. 'It's all quick-quick and hush-hush, over before it started. We don't want to wake up the kids.'

'Hm,' I say, surprised a little that Jane could conceivably also be after some fun, 'that sucks. Let's see what we can do about that tonight?' I lift my head up to look at her, and a strand of black hair gently slaps my face. I grin. 'Maybe we could get a bit Luze?'

Jane laughs out loud, 'You are incorrigible.' But she likes it, and there is a feeling in the air that life, at least tonight, is limitless in its possibilities.

Jane was married and pregnant six months later, and Manjit was a history. She married a bespectacled Andrew, who was a bit shorter than her, and she no longer had to be an au pair. Some you win, and some you lose. Sometimes, you choose. Other times, it chooses you.

At Jane's tiny little wedding party, I wondered why she was so set on getting married. Was this an id, or was it an ego? Was she hooked by her past? And why was I apparently so against settling down, whatever that meant? This made me think of Peter. He wanted me to settle down. I have been trying not to think about Peter, and it worked quite well, for the most part. But then, your past hooks you, and sooner or later, it reels you back in.

Back in Prague, he stayed longer than the two weeks he had planned. He injured himself while training, and he didn't get to go to the Games. This was a terrible blow, but they say things happen for a reason. A psychoanalyst might even suggest that he wanted to injure himself because there were other things he wanted or needed to do more. Although sometimes, arguably, a cigar is just a cigar.

In any event, I was there to see him through it. We saw each other every day and we walked holding hands. We drank too much, I danced, he watched, we stayed up late, we listened to music, and we had sex in previously unimagined places. We both loved this city with its cobbled streets, and nothing could stop us. Or so we thought. You do when you are eighteen. And we talked. I couldn't believe I had this much to say to one person. Maybe it was me who was nostalgic for something Slovakian.

Peter liked holding hands, and even though it wasn't my thing, I didn't take my hand away. Maybe that was a mistake. Holding hands carried a promise I was still not ready to make.

During my psychology A-level, I read a bit of Lacan for Beginners, and from the little, I could understand of it, if I did, Lacan thought we learn what we want by wanting what the other wants. It made sense to me when I watched my five-year-old cousin with her sibling. Or two dogs under the same roof. They always want what the other one wants. And, if someone wants us, they actually want us to want them – so we do. Sometimes. I actually think no one really knows what Lacan really meant, but you could keep at it infinitely. Forever in search of something lost, which we never had. An attempt to recapture something, some sense of oneness. When you want for nothing, like before you knew that the image in the mirror was you, before you realised you are separate from the world surrounding you and in fact, quite alone. Anyway, when I was with Peter back then, a lot of the time, it felt like we were one. When someone wants you to want them really badly, and your personal universe approves, desire is born. How does a desire for the desire of the other end? It gets killed.

That is the order of things. That day Peter came to meet me after work, I knew we would not be going to see the band playing in Café Rouge. He said he had something to show me and passed me a letter. How do we know the moment the end arrives? When something is being passed to us that we know won't taste good? The letter was stamped from Slovakia. His father wrote, and it was as short as the shortest straw you can draw. His mother wasn't well. Could he come back. Peter wanted me to go with him.

Meet his parents, stay with him, find a home and carry on having sex in places previously unimagined. And all the rest of it. But I couldn't do that. Go back. It didn't just feel like going back. It felt like going backwards. Too much like settling down. Settling down for what? I didn't know.

He said, 'M. Please don't do this.' It's annoying when you hear it, and you realise it's not the first time. It's like a really bad romance novel or something. But there was no going back for me. So I left. But not before we drank and smoked the evening away. I was too drunk. We had sex in the pub's disabled toilet, not a place either of us imagined as a venue for the leaving party, a wake for the desire killed. The story of desire that started the night Veronika's hair caught on fire. It's as if we knew it wouldn't last from the beginning. Maybe that was what made the insatiability so present.

After, I said, 'bye, Peter' with a quick hug, and then I walked out of the pub into the cold night. Stepping back into my life going forward, the dark street lit only by the old Victorian lamps. It was snowing so no one could tell what was snow and what were tears on my face. That was also the night I went back to my flat to find out I was homeless. Some days, life is like that.

That was then. It is more than a year ago now, but it still feels like guilt or regret when I think about it, even though Leith came after Peter. Did I have to leave? Was it ID, or was it the ego that made that decision? What was I repeating? Why do I always have to leave? Was I Luse, or was I Lost? Sitting in my little au-pair bedroom, vaguely listening to the hushed argument between Paul and Angela behind the thin walls, I feel a familiar restlessness. Angela is fed up, and I don't blame her. She wants to move to Australia, but Paul won't hear of it as he thinks it will jeopardise his acting career. 'What fucking career?' I hear Angela hiss and silently applaud her. The thing in jeopardy was their marriage, but Paul couldn't see it. It will come as a surprise to him one day.

I have finished my final year of learning English as a Foreign Language. The girls that I have been friendly with are going back to where they came from, although hopefully bringing something with them to enrich the bleak tapestry of the Eastern Bloc. There is nothing left to do in east London now. Time to move. Again.

Working as an au pair has been fun but I am bored of Paul and Angela's unresolved issues playing out in front of us all. Apart from his fetish for dressing up, which is paradoxically the only real thing about Paul, they keep pretending to live their lives like adults- but they are just two scared, angry kids who don't even like each other that much. Stuck together, hooked by the past, thrashing about helplessly, reeled back and forth, not looking back, just blindly keeping on going, doing the same over and over. It will probably end in an affair. It will be Angela who leaves, that would be my bet. I have seen this sort of thing before, except the original version was darker. I was five when I stood between my father, incoherent with rage, and my mother, who was so drunk she was swaying on the spot, eyes glazed, not seeing, not hearing. Not seeing, not hearing her daughter, who was screaming so loudly she wouldn't have a voice in the morning. Mad kind of screaming to try to distract father from hurting her mother. He looked like he was going to kill her. Paul isn't going to kill Angela, but the feel of this house's song is not easy-listening. Too familiar, too close to home and yet no home at all. Time to go.

Recently, I met a new guy. A nice guy. He is handsome, lean and muscular, with an outlook on life I don't understand so it intrigues me. He wears light blue ripped-at-the-knees jeans that try to hide his thighs and hang off his backside like his attitude, relaxed and attractive. He is from New Zealand. I never met anyone from there before, and it sounds like another planet. He wears a flannel check shirt, and he thinks most people are good. He also believes that all people should be given the benefit of the doubt. Maybe New Zealand *is* another planet. We met in an Irish bar, which at the stroke of midnight, in some reverse Cinderella manoeuvre, becomes a nightclub. His name is Don.

CHAPTER 10
MORE ABOUT THE GUY I MET IN AN IRISH PUB

EAST LONDON, 1999

The wedding and the issue of roots

Once I was a rain. Beating at your windows.

But you didn't hear. So I left on the leaves of a rhododendron at my silky leisure.

Dissolving. Time and again. Time after time. How long do you have.

Then I was a sea. A strong swimmer, you didn't drown.

But now I couldn't see you. Wood for trees, you can't see tears for seas.

In your eyes, on your face, washing away.

Pain. Shame. Name it.

And then, I was a river. A stream unclogged.

Waited to be released. To flow into myself.

I've been there all along.

Waiting for you.

The house in which Don was renting a room was like a warren, with many secret nooks and crannies. His room was carpeted, with a single bed, a bedside table with nightlight, a writing desk with a reading lamp, and an old single wardrobe with a matching chest of drawers. Unlike the house outside his room, it was orderly and practical. Like Don. We never made it upstairs the first time I came over. It couldn't wait. It was too urgent to find each other in the privacy of four walls. In some senses, Don could leave his practical side aside.

I went back to his on our second date, and it wasn't romantic. Romantic sex seemed to me an oxymoron, a very unsexy idea. We were downstairs, on the squeaky wooden floor that was, like us, barely dressed in the worn-out Persian carpet, in this house with many rooms. Good things often come at some cost. Carpet burns can be one of them.

We moved in together six months later. I found myself in a novel position. I didn't want to leave.

Don rents a room in Christian's house with Sam and Pascal. Sam's girlfriend, Gretchen, stays there most weekends and a few days a week. The house is one of those terraced semi-detached creatures, in a solid row of them, on a street that looks like the one next to it and the one after that, in spreading colonies of rows snaking across London's less wealthy suburbia.

It's six in the evening, and Don is playing the drums to a rhythm that is only apparent to him. Sam is rolling a joint that's ungainly and too long, and Gretchen is singing even though she can't. I am on a flowery French two-seater dented in everybody's shape, ungainly like the joint Sam is rolling. I am smoking a cigarette and trying to read Solzhenitsyn's *Cancer Ward*. I feel disheartened about the man's magic with words. His book fell on deaf ears in terms of its politics and its underlying message, but it captured hearts at least, which is something. It is more than can be said for a lot of things. Christian is working on an image of a mythical bird; he is glass etching, using some acidic substance to roughen the texture of the surface of the glass. This is his seventh bird. He likes things to be around him. The more things, the merrier. He is in another room, only slightly shielded from the indomitable cigarette smoke, which you can see everywhere even if you can see through it, and it doesn't care if it offends. Christian doesn't smoke anymore but he doesn't mind the smoke circling around the people and things, leisurely and suave like James Bond.

The front door bangs in the familiar double beat, and presently, Pascal comes in, shaking off the wet umbrella onto the unsuspecting floor, making that happy noise you do when you step inside a warm room from a wet cold outside, shaking yourself off like a dog that got drenched. He has been to some exhibition and says, you should see it, M, it is very wonderful. Pascal is French.

It is a Saturday, and everyone is happy. We won't be tomorrow; the Sunday sadness is a thing, but tomorrow feels a long way away, and we are never thinking about tomorrow on Saturdays. Who does when they are twenty-one. Pascal is a French supply teacher. He comes from a nice family in Paris and, I reckon, has probably never seen a shithole like Tanning Town School, where he teaches French to children who can barely speak their own tongue. He is taking it in his stoic stride, though and looks charmed by it. Perhaps this is a thing about the French. They can seem charmed by the weirdest of things. Or maybe it is a Pascal thing.

Sam walks over with the joint. 'My friend, this will be the best you ever tasted,' he says in his midlands drawl after a sharp inhale, holding his breath to let the magic penetrate his lungs and bloodstream before the cough comes to warn him in vain.

'*Mon Dieu*', Pascal smiles broadly as he cheerfully accepts this peace pipe and takes a drag on it like the world's peace depends on it, '*C'est Magnifique!*'

They talk about music, if you can call it talk. It sounds more like the sound of Nemo trapped inside the belly of the whale. Pascal plays the cello in a small band he had put together. Sam only plays on my nerves, but he can talk about most things like he knows what he is talking about. There is a name for it; I read it somewhere recently- the *Dunning-Kruger effect*. A psychological phenomenon when an individual with low ability or knowledge in a specific area overestimates their competence. I put down Solzhenitsyn and look for the magazine under the living room table. Here it goes. "They may lack the awareness to recognise their own limitations, leading them to believe they know more than they actually do." A bit like Greek *hubris*. To think we kissed that first night. I squirm at the random funny luck of it. Thank God that's all we did. The smell of marijuana and the men's talk are washing over me like a lullaby. I feel relaxed. I love being here. I come at weekends and some weeknights but I am still looking after other people's children for living, so I need to be back to take them to school in the morning. Coming here feels good. It is like a Wonderland, this house, busting at the seams with things. We are all here from different places in the world, in different shapes and with different angles, but somehow, we all come together in this picture of 44 Godwin Road, and the composition works. It is probably because of Christian. A father figure to us all, in one way or another. A man who was adopted is now a caregiver.

Christian owns the house. He used to live here with his wife, who left him for a man who wanted to have children. Christian, despite what his name might suggest, could not be less religious if he tried, but if he was walking in Memphis and got asked, "Tell me, are you a Christian child?" he would say, "Ma'am, I am tonight." He went to a Quaker school. He has been at Tanning Town School for nearly thirty years, probably to repent for some sin he unconsciously imagined he committed when he was abandoned by his natural mother and got adopted by a nice, well-to-do family. His father is called Roy, which would, in my mind, forever remain a name connected with moneyed Surrey if it wasn't for the day I met another Roy. This Roy was a shady criminal defence solicitor, previously a shady police officer, who would sometimes sleep under his desk, stinking of booze and the stale cigarette butts in the ashtray next to him, listening to Bob Dylan on an old cassette player. Roys come in all shapes and sizes. Roy, the Surreyed one, is married to Barbara, and they speak in that 1940s BBC radio broadcast accent. It is mesmerising to me, how they bend letters and words into sounds so different to the others living in the same country, speaking the same language. Christian can, at the drop of his adopted posh hat, take or leave the accent behind, which he has to each day as he enters his classroom at the Tanning Town School.

'A top up, Shmeli?' he walks over with his Chianti Classico that cost five pounds in the off-licence shop down the road, and is unlikely to be either a Chianti or a Classico. He adds 'sh' to my name to honour the many 'shs' in my Slavic tongue.

'Don't mind if I do,' I say, to honour his adopted father's ancestry and the catchphrase of Colonel Humphrey Chinstrap on the 1940s British radio comedy.

Everyone feels at home at Christian's; you can feel it, and we all know it is a special thing we have here. In a constant embrace by all the things that surround us, collected for the sheer pleasure of being looked at, touched and talked about. Maybe, when you are adopted, you like to adopt things. All these things in the world that might otherwise not have a home. I said in my letter to Veronika that maybe things are changing. For example, I really like Don's hands. I also like thinking about Don's hands. They are big, warm, and strong. My hand, in his hand, I am in good hands. I wait for his calls impatiently. All day, I wait for the moment the phone goes rrrrrrrring, and I don't care about seeing other people. I see Jane less, and my circle of friends is shifting to reshape into a form around Don's friends. This should all be alarming, but it isn't. What "should be" is currently under review. Don has something about him that has a constant pull on me. Even if I wanted to, which I don't, I couldn't be too far away from him for too long. Like a solid tree Don is grounded, adjusted to his new climate, and he has roots. You can't see them, but you can feel them. He looks like he can never topple. And you like to sit by him.

I look up from the book, watching him beat the drums, a look of stoned concentration on his face. It looks like sleep with a nice dream in it, but then he pauses, sticks hanging in the air, noise suspended for a second it takes for him to meet my eye; he mouths, 'alright?' I nod and smile, and he smiles back and returns the sticks to the drums to the beat that is undiscernible, with his eyes closed. Because that's how you best hear music.

We order a curry later. The boys go for the spicy, the girls for the colour. We finish the wine, and all of us, at some point in time, make for our den, content in a way that I have never imagined myself being capable of.

'We used to have this big cherry tree in our garden,' I am saying to Don, looking at the line of tall trees separating the road from the large swathes of green land, surrounded by a neat line of uniform houses. 'Well, at least it used to feel big.' We are walking home from our local pub, hand in hand, while our childhood memories are putting up their own hands, wanting to be known - *me, Miss, me!* 'I used to climb up really high so that I couldn't hear them. And sit there and eat all the cherries until my stomach ached, and I would have to stop.'

He doesn't say anything. I worry I said too much.

'They were the shiniest things.' I say, remembering how perfectly red they were, the tiny shards of light refracting from their smooth surface. They could have been made of glass. They looked like a work of art. I can't remember the taste though; it's a long time ago, and the taste is overwritten by some other memory. 'Did you use to climb trees?' I ask.

'Yes, I did. And I also used to eat cherries.' He says and smiles at me. It is a gentle smile that could be a beginning of a joke, a gentle tease or, it could be leaving me space to say more.

'You don't like talking about trees?' I ask, not smiling.

'I am happy to talk about trees. It is just that you are lucky this was not your chat-up line.' He puts his arm around my shoulder and pulls me into him, kissing my cold face until it doesn't feel cold anymore. The evening is calm, and the only noise I can hear is the trees and the wind playing their Sunday night piece.

'Is there anything else about the trees you would like to tell me?' Don says once he releases me. He knows when he is onto something, but he doesn't force his way in, and that makes it feel lighter to let him.

'Yes. Well, not trees. Cherries. I never used to eat cherries which had a crack in the skin.' I am serious and I am looking at my feet touching the pavement to ground myself. Can he take it? Will he run away when he knows how cracked my own surface is?

'Why?' No more teasing in there. The leaves quiet down as if to encourage me like the chorus in a Greek tragedy. *Go on, M, go on, you can trust him, tell him, tell him.*

'Because you never know what made the crack. And there could be something inside them you might bite into. And then, that knowledge never leaves you. Of having bitten into something disgusting, living, you know, it leaves a bad taste in your mouth. You can't exactly halve a cherry and inspect it. Not while you are sitting on a branch of the tree, anyway.' I suddenly think I have spent all my life so far sitting on a branch of the tree.

'Like what?'

'What like what?'

'Like what could be in it?'

'A maggot. A living squirming writhing maggot. God, I hate maggots.'

'Maggots don't eat cherries, I don't think. It's some kind of worm, probably some larvae of the cherry fruit fly?' Don says thoughtfully. Adding, 'That would make sense, actually, they probably lay eggs on the cherries...' warming up to his theme, before looking up and then stopping, seeing my face that doesn't lie.

I say, 'That's good to know.' Dry as a bone.

'Sorry,' Don says, remorsefully enough. 'I just thought you might want to know...'

'Nope,' I say, 'maggots or worms, whatever, they are wrong to be there, and they are hideous.'

'Yes, they are pretty unpleasant,' Don agrees, understatedly.

'Don. It's not *unpleasant.* Unpleasant is a taste of milk that's going off. Or, the English weather. The experience of a maggot-worm in a beautiful cherry is of seeing something healthy being devoured by something beastly. Tiny but beastly, squirming, gnawing away at the beautiful thing inside out, destroying it. That's systemic warfare, not *unpleasant.*'

'A tiny beast warfare…' Don starts to speak, but I have started now, and I have not finished yet.

'And do you know what gets me about it the most? The deceit of it. The insidious thing inside can't be seen from the outside. So you can't tell what is going on. Until it's too late. That's why you have to look out for the cracks on the surface.' I sound nuts. I will freak him out. What am I doing. I smile a small, unsure smile that seems to be saying *I am not completely mad,* and also, it implies a possibility that I am just joking, being light-hearted. But who am I trying to fool? Myself, probably.

'M, but you do know, don't you, that not all cherries have an ugly thing inside them.' Don says quietly, beginning to understand how big his job will be.

'Yes. However, the Problem with a capital P is that you can't tell by looking at them. And once you bite into them, it's too late. It becomes a part of you, and you can't ever really get it out of your mind, even if you get it out of your gut. So, you really need to make sure you pick your cherries carefully. *Mon cheri.*' I smile, lightness finding a way back in.

'Hm, I see.' Don says, and I love him for it. 'Well, I don't mind if cherries have a few little cracks in them. Or, even if they are a little bit bad.' He carries on, expanding the metaphor, making the hay while the light is shining.

Well, that's just as fucking well, I think to myself while I hear myself say, 'Or mad. You think I am mad now.'

'Not now.' He disagrees. 'I already knew it when you and Sam met.' He doesn't at all looked alarmed by my maggot madness or the fact that his best friend briefly dated me before him. Briefly and nearly are important adjectives when it comes to assessing the scale of any invasion. And if something nearly happened, it didn't happen at all.

I kiss him. It's not a big kiss. There is nothing overly romance-like going on here; it just feels like a beautiful butterfly landed on my arm and I want to behold the moment. Not take my eyes off it. It is a thank you kiss. Don is the closest to a perfect cherry I have ever seen. And I have been looking.

'Did you go up there often?' he asks me gently, as if by the by, referring to the other part of the story I revealed about myself earlier. He hasn't forgotten. He never does.

'Quite often.' We are approaching the house now. Alison Moyet is being Weak in the Presence of Beauty, and Christian is cooking a roast tonight. Sundays don't always feel like Sundays. Maybe today, we are all cried out.

Don doesn't ask what I did when the cherries were not in season. Where did I go to escape what I didn't want to hear or be around? Or who were the real-life maggots, and why did I fear having internalised them? How could they make me feel so bad? Whose were these little squirming demons, really, and why did I not just spit them out? Instead of letting them eat away at me all this time, driving me from tree to tree, from one relationship to another, all my life like a hopping epiphyte that thinks everything is her fault. Having internalised somebody else's guilt. Never putting my roots down. He now knows a little bit about why I have been leaving places all my life. I wonder what that might feel like for him. Will I just up and leave if I start to feel unsafe again? Unsafe means Unloved.

'M?' he says, stopping me gently from fully opening the door.

I look up at him, close up, he is right there, and I am beginning to really like the way his face can do that thing, go from fun to serious and back to light again, dependably, always returning to light. 'Yes?'

'There are worse things than maggots.' He says as if that was supposed to reassure me somehow.

'What are we talking, like being dead?' I joke. Or at least I think I joke.

'Being dead at fifteen.' Don says, and then he opens the door and gives my arm a squeeze, and I want to say wait, but don't.

We walk through the small porch, which has Michaelangelo's poster on the ceiling, and I am not sure if the squeeze is to punctuate the end of The Previously Untold Story of an Old Cherry Tree or if it is the beginning of another one.

A few weeks later, I will find out that Don lost a friend when he was fifteen in a terrible accident at the rugby pitch when his friend tripped over a live wire. This will be the first story we will unpick together, getting a look at the invisible worm that gnawed away at Don's heart once. He just told me that night because he wanted me to know he knew what it felt like to have something eating at you from inside. And that things could always be worse but now they were good, and that was what really mattered.

It's Summer, and we are in a little Italian restaurant. I always have the same thing here. Lasagne with a glass of red. The lasagne costs only five pounds, and it's divine. I am eating the hot meal, burning my mouth because it's too good to wait and I am starving, when Don says, with a serious Don face,

'M. Will you always love me?'

I swallow my mouthful slowly this time. How can I know that?

But I say, 'Yes,' because it doesn't seem like the right time for a philosophical answer. And, 'Why?' although my stomach knows the answer because it is doing somersaults.

'Shall we get married?'

'I think so.' I say but don't say, if you will have me, and, are you sure.

'Ok.'

'Are you asking me because my visa is running out?'

'No. I am asking you because I want to spend the rest of my life with you. But, it will help the visa situation, too.' Says my orderly, practical husband-to-be Don.

He had said recently, that he wanted to spend the rest of his life with me. We were with a friend in the North Star, our local pub. I was shocked then because if I was to admit it to myself, I still found it hard to believe I could be loved. Loved like that, really loved, not just utilised in some way or another, in a mutually satisfying set of circumstances. I was also shocked that I was letting myself believe it, breaking up with my policy of being a girl with no roots, and shocked that he would say it so openly, not caring if the whole world was listening. Not that the world ever listens anywhere near as much as people might imagine. And also, how could he possibly know that he wanted to spend the rest of his life with me? It could be a long prison sentence. But Don knew things I did not.

'Me too.' I said because my stomach believed it.

For the next few months of my life, I stopped walking. Instead of walking, I danced along. I danced every step of the way. There was music in my head and lightness in my feet and in my soul and I have never before felt like this. He would actually marry me. He actually really loved me. He actually wanted to spend the rest of his life with me. The rest of your life feels like a really long time when you are at the beginning.

When I was with Don, I felt like I could be myself. I didn't know exactly who that was, but this new me felt like a real thing. A good thing. I wasn't the same girl who left her country, a maelstrom in her head, into the land of the Unknown, thrown around the place like Dorothy in the storm. Back then, in Prague, I had no idea about the Yellow Brick Road.

Should I Stay or Should I Go was one of the songs that played all the time in Jo's, but for a while, this Dorothy had no say in the matter – the storm was taking me places like a wild horse might an inexperienced cowboy, until one day, I found out the reins were in my hands all along. It was Don who showed me.

He held my hands in his warm and steady hold until his love passed through them, an electric current delivering the bloodline supply of his belief in goodness into my very core until, one day, it became a part of me, too. Every time he held my hand in his, I felt it. Something is building itself up, layer by layer. It was weak to begin with and fell time and again, like a house of cards, for a long time, but he wasn't worried. He had so much goodness in him that he could never run out. Every time he held my hand, I fell in love with him a little bit more. Over and again, I was learning to trust, like a child learns to talk. It was a new language. And English had nothing to do with it.

We married two months later. It was a hot summer day, a week before my birthday. The best gift I would ever get. A lifetime of Don.

CHAPTER 11
I AM GETTING READY TO SLAY THE SEVEN-HEADED DRAGON

NEW ZEALAND, 2025

How many fatherly slaps are too many?

It is nearly time to visit a place people usually call "back home". It is a place which, for me, never felt like home because home should feel nice, not like falling into a raccoon den. This is the first time since we have been together that Don is not coming with me. It is a long way to go for two weeks. It is a long way to go to put myself in a bad mood. Don said, 'How many more times do you need to get hurt by the miserable prick before you realise you don't have to do that anymore.' He doesn't say it before I go. He will say it when I call him in tears from Slovakia a few weeks later when the miserable prick will hurt me again. Don could sometimes get angry.

The miserable prick wasn't always miserable. There was a time before I discovered language, before I learned that things around me had names and meanings, a time when my father would smile at me, and I would smile back. That's what humans do; they mimic each other. The mimicking gets a bit more sophisticated with time, people forever want what the other wants, but it starts with a smile. Or a frown, you get the idea. During this time Before Language, when I happily believed that things and I were one and the same, that I was at one with the universe, as babies must feel they are, not knowing their skin is a boundary between them and the world of things, my father would smile, and he would be gentle. I wouldn't have believed it, and I don't remember it because you don't exactly remember things that happen before you have words, because you have no way of attaching a story to the memory, but there was a photo of it. He used to carry a black and white photograph of me and him in his wallet for a long time. I don't know when he stopped, but one day, it just wasn't there anymore. In the photo, I am a six-month-old little human, lying on his stomach, content and trusting. He is wearing a floral shirt, a hangover from the 60s; everything came late in communist Europe if it ever arrived. His face separated into two with a dark line of moustache. He had a shoulder length, black, wavy hair then. He is smiling in the photo, looking at me with what seems softness in his eyes. And I look like an ordinary, curious baby.

But that was a long time ago. The image feels incongruous and unreal. Our smiles are not available anymore. They, too, stopped who knows when, but if I had to pick a time, it was likely the time when he first turned his rage towards me, not satisfied anymore with only beating up the mother every now and then. When she "sure as God deserved it."

When I was around eight, I sneaked a bunch of homemade chorizo from the pantry and took it to school to ingratiate myself with a teacher I was scared of. He went mad. Someone must have told him before I got home because he was ready for me.

Then, there was another time when I was about ten. I went out after school with my friend. I went out despite him saying no because he grounded me for something so stupid I forgot what it was. I didn't forget the slap. It burnt my skin, and it etched itself into my soul. I was walking unsuspecting, talking to my friend, when she saw him jump out of the car at quite some distance and start walking towards us, fast. I knew it wouldn't be good when he reached us. When he caught up with me, the blow came so fast I didn't even see it coming. His hand hit hard, and it hurt. Not just the physical pain. That was the least of it. It was the humiliation. The helplessness. I could do nothing. I could do absolutely nothing back. Nothing about it. Nothing to him. He hurt me, probably feeling all of those things himself. Humiliated by a ten-year-old. Helpless against her growing up and away. And, scared. I think we were both scared of each other, but I didn't know it then. Any of it. All I knew was the rage inside me. I still draw on it to this day when I need to.

When I stole the chocolate bar in the local supermarket, I must have started to know some things. I was becoming more desperate. Desperate to alert the world that my father was not right, not right in the head, and my mother wasn't doing anything about it. But the world doesn't much care. It has too much on its plate. Not enough resources.

The shame you bring on us. Stealing now, are we? You will be my ruin. I will beat it out of you, mark my words. With each hit, he taught me. The rage erupting Vesuvius-like, I wasn't sure I would survive this one. There was no more the man from the photo. Not one tiny molecule of him left. Where did he go? Why did he leave? What happened to that man? And the silent mother who let all the slaps come and wouldn't make them go. One day, one day, I promised myself, again and again, each hit a ringing endorsement, making myself believe one day I would be free from this. Surely.

That day came in 1994. I was seventeen. I stayed calm even though the slap was burning my cheek in a now familiar pattern, and tears wanted to come. But, at that moment- and you know it when it arrives, it greets you silently like a distant relative you didn't know you had. I just knew this was the last time. Just knew it. It happens with humans. You push them all the way they will go. And then, when there is no more go left in them, they either break or they rise up, like the giant swell of water, and push back. And that's when the pusher gets scared. I looked at my father steadily. I could feel the ice in my glare like it was in my heart. I have grown a shield.

'This will never happen again,' I said, so calm, it was as if someone else was speaking for me. 'I'm leaving.' I watched him, and I held his eye until he knew I meant it.

He laughed, 'Oh, yeah? Good luck. Just tell me this, where will you go?'

I said, 'Anywhere. I will literally go anywhere to get away from here.'

When he realised I wasn't bluffing, his tone changed, malicious and snake-like, his last attempt at scaring me.

'You think you have it all figured out, don't you? You think you are so fucking smart. Well, let's see who will have the last laugh.'

'I'm not laughing.'

Then I left and never came back.

Did he take pleasure in all that pain? And humiliation? I never asked him. And now it doesn't seem a good time. He is eighty, and his now all-too-visible ageing makes it seem cruel to ask about the man he once was. Parkinson's is ravaging what's left of his mind and of his will to live, which has never been a glass half full. I sometimes wonder if he has waited for this moment all his life. To be old. Some strive to live their lives; some wait them out. Only a few sleeps to go before my visit. I am going with Hermione. The half term is only two weeks and there is no point in us all going – too expensive, not long enough. Also, very, very long and not expensive enough to be able to say, I can't justify it. How much is too much to go and visit your ailing father living in another country? Burt will be going with Don on a road trip to the South Island to visit his well-adjusted, kind and lovely grandparents. It is too expensive to fly all of us across the world for too short a time, for no good time at all.

People say, "I am so sorry to hear that, is he ok?" when I answer the question of why I am going back "home" so soon after our move here. On hearing about his Parkinsons and his health decline, people say things they assume to be the correct things to say for the circumstances. They are mainly things to fill in awkward gaps where the only true thing left to say is nothing nice. Sometimes, there is nothing nice left to say, but people find that hard to accept. So they throw stuff at it, approximately hitting the target board.

And I don't tell the truth either. I don't say, 'No, he is not ok. And he is only going to get worse. Not better.' Nor do I say, 'I'm ok with it, you know. That's life, right? And he hasn't always been very nice, so I didn't hang out with him much once I had a choice.' I can't say this to these people who say, "I am so sorry to hear that. Is he ok." You just don't. Unless you don't like them, but you don't talk about your father (whom you struggle to like) to people you don't like. Just not the thing. Like a double negative. Will it be the last time, I wonder. Will it be the last time I will get to see my father? And does it matter? It must matter, but I don't know what to do with knowing this. It's one whole life. It's the life of one man that is coming to an end. A man who has been in my life all my life, in one way or another. No matter how far I went, he followed in my mind, with me, everywhere I went. Not that he has always been *on* my mind. Far from it. But he always lurked in there. He made me suspicious of humans; he made me doubt my own goodness. He made me believe I didn't deserve good things.

But he, unwittingly, also made me strong. And perceptive to the point I felt, at times, I could read people's minds like they were an open book. And my rage has been a lifetime endurance supply in the moments when nothing else would have seen me through.

For some reason, I remember our old living room. The last time we were there we made a song and dance about his birthday, he was seventy. There was, of course, no dancing and no singing. Don, me and the kids gathered in the gloom of my parents' classic 1970s living room furniture, still shiny. Some hinges were worn and creaky, but you wouldn't have known it was over fifty years old. Unless you knew. They were all well looked after. I think that when you love things, you wear them out a bit, and that's ok. When you are scared of things, they may remain pristine, but they are also untouched by a human soul. They remain, stand still and proud, a memorial to fear.

I am brought back to my current life by a sound emanating beside me, somewhere in between the bed covers and pillows and the two dogs, 'Mum…?' followed by a pause to check Hermione has my full attention. She is in my bed, reading a book.

'Yes, Hermione.'

'Do you even love him?' apropos of nothing as she does.

'Your dad?' trying to keep it away from where it's inexorably going.

'No. Your dad.'

I don't want to lie, and I don't know the truth. What do you do then? 'It's complicated, but, yes, in some way.' I say after a moment, during which Hermione patiently waits. Adding, 'I thought you were reading.'

'I wouldn't love him if I were you.' Hermione says, ignoring half of my response. She knows that my father has been a very strict parent. What she doesn't know, she senses. And her senses are extraordinary.

'As I say, it's complicated. I don't exactly like him, but I understand how he came to be the way he is, and that makes me less unforgiving and a bit more capable of loving.' Sometimes, I don't say. Sometimes, I can forgive and love him. Other times, I will never be able to.

'Well, I think you are a very kind person. I hope one day I will be like you. Kind, cool and pretty.' And she moves closer and puts her little arms around my waist and her head now rests on my stomach.

'In between the times when I am the worst parent ever, and you hate me, and you wish you were adopted?' I say, smile in my eyes, twisting a strand of my daughter's blond hair around my fingers. I love Hermione's hair; it's soft, and yet it has an attitude. Like her.

'We are not talking about the past, Mum. We are talking about now. You need to learn to take a compliment, Mum.'

I do. I do need to learn to accept a nice thing being said about me to me and not bat it back, unsure of its intended recipient or if it was meant to be a gift or a hit. I embrace my daughter, trying not to bend her neck too much before she says Mum, remember I have a neck? And I hold her tight and whispers into her hair, 'I do, Hermione, you are right.'

'I am always right, Mum. And you are the best mum in the world. Funny, crazy Mum. Can we do some baking?' and then, still in my arms, 'Do you remember that time you set the cupcakes on fire when Burt's friend was over to play?'

'I try not to.'

'Don't worry, Mum, you can't be good at everything.'

Don walks in, followed by Burt and says, 'No, that's true. That's my thing.' And he falls onto the bed with us like a giant teddy bear, and Burt jumps on top like a rumbustious monkey let loose and for a moment, everything is as it should be.

Later, when I am in the shower, warm water soothing on my back, I remember someone saying you have your best thoughts in a warm shower. What I was thinking just a moment ago was that I couldn't imagine slapping my children. I don't know what made me think about this, but I wonder if these are my best thoughts. I imagine, with some pleasure being able to occasionally tell them to just piss off and leave me the fuck alone for five minutes, and it would undoubtedly feel energising to do so. The shock of incredulity on their faces alone would be worth it. But, to use physical force on a human half my size can't be right and shouldn't be imaginable. It makes me think of those nature documentaries where a lion catches and kills a baby antelope. You just don't like it; you watch, hoping for a miracle, even though you know that it is just a part of the circle of life, and if lions never caught food, they would die out. Or, different but the same, when a man with a rifle shoots a bunny. Or, he trains his dogs to brutalise foxes, or he shoots ducks who just want to quack and be happy. It just doesn't feel right.

There is a discrepancy, the inequality of power, the gaping lack of humaneness in the act. Things should be free to live without having to cower. It's a basic *humane* right. Because only then you can grow to your full height. I read recently that up until the 18th century, we spelt "human" as "humane". I wonder what it did for the humaneness of humanity.

But there is always another side to the coin. Say, you watched the documentary following the lion on its journey from a cub to becoming a young lion man, then the act of his first kill might feel like a moment of pride. So, it's all about context. And survival. In the case of the lion, survival is about not dying from starvation. In my father's case, survival is about maintaining the illusion of control. He survived, psychically, by trying to control, which is to say, coerce, his immediate environment lest a revolution broke out in his own home. And he saw it. He saw it forming in the small body of his wilful daughter. His fear that I might expose him for who he was and then They would be after him. I mean I have no idea of what kind of dark stuff he suspected of himself, but it was a heavy charge, I have no doubt. I have no doubt because he projected it onto me, and I carried it for a long time.

I increase the temperature of the water, and as I do, I remember a passage from Solzhenitsyn's *Cancer Ward*, where he describes one of his characters, the contemptible, sad administrative creature called Rusanov. His job was to collect data on all people for one purpose only. To terrorise their dreams. Manipulate them and get them to do what they were told. I turn the water as cold as I can bear before I turn off the shower and towel myself down. Wrapped in my cosy bathrobe, I walk over to my bookshelf to find the passage in the book to remind myself what I am thinking about. This is one of the reasons I highlight things when I read. To be able to return to them.

"It was a job that went by different names in different institutions, but the substance of it was always the same. Only ignoramuses and uninformed outsiders were unaware of what subtle, meticulous work it was, and what talent it required. It was a form of poetry not yet mastered by the poets themselves. As every man goes through life, he fills in a number of forms for the record, each containing a number of questions. A man's answer to one question on one form becomes a little thread, permanently connecting him to the local centre of personnel records administration. There are thus hundreds of little threads radiating from every man, millions of threads in all. If these threads were suddenly to become visible, the whole sky would look like a spider's web, and if they materialized as elastic bands, buses, trams, and even people would all lose the ability to move, and the wind would be unable to carry torn-up newspapers or autumn leaves along the streets of the city.

They are not visible; they are not material, but every man is constantly aware of their existence. The point is that a so-called completely clean record was almost unattainable, an ideal, like absolute truth. Something negative or suspicious can always be noted down against any man alive. Everyone is guilty of something or has something to conceal. All one has to do is to look hard enough to find out what it is.

Each man, permanently aware of his own invisible threads, naturally develops a respect for the people who manipulate the threads, who manage personnel records administration, that most complicated science, and for these people's authority."

In my father's day, turning coats was about survival. My father's day was a day in which history was daily overwritten by ideology, and the non-compliance with which could easily see you marched off to a Siberian camp, and not many returned from there. I suspect my father wasn't only a cub who didn't know a mother's gentle touch or his father's stern eye ever softening, but he also lived in fear all his life.

Fear may be a decent governess, but it is not a bedfellow you want to spend your life with.

'Mum?' Burt pokes his head around the corner of the bathroom door. I am back in there because it is the only place in the house I can lock the door on; if I remember, and today is not that day.

'Yes, Burtie.'

'I have a proposal to make.' It's not how Burt speaks, but he is trying it on. It might fit his purpose. We have been talking about the way in which he asks for things. Like me, Burt is somewhere on the spectrum, and being less conditioned by social expectations due to his age makes the construct of politeness an issue as it makes the issue of telling the truth a virtue. In a family where most people speak their thoughts with little to no screening, his requests often sound like commands, and it doesn't bode well. Not in a family where no one likes to be told what to do.

'Can it wait until I finish in here…'

But Burt is already speaking, seated on the closed toilet in the corner of my bathroom. He wants to earn money to buy tokens in some electronic game. He proposes to do a list of things which never in a million years would pay the kind of money he is asking for, except for this very year, in this very house, by this very mother. His parameters are shaped by his parents' ability to make something out of nothing much. His understanding of the value of things is similarly predisposed. It is a troubling dilemma. You don't want to deprive your kids because you were once deprived. Yet you want them to understand the cost and the value of things, ideally in the right order. You also don't want to force things on your kids that you wished for as a kid that they couldn't care less about but might feel obliged to do to please you. It is a lot. It is a lot to get right, and it is a lot to get wrong. Either way, they will blame you.

'So, you want to earn real money to buy pretend money. Is that right?' I say as I remove my eye makeup from one of my eyes, resigning myself to the fact that my me-time is over for tonight. There is no point. Good thoughts and all thoughts are gone to another home.

'Yes, but I don't like how you make it sound.'

'I sound it exactly like it is. You want my money to buy pretend money, which you are going to spend on something you will never be able to physically hold in your hand.'

'Stop it, Mum.' I stay silent as I wipe off the eye makeup from the other eye. I can see his small shoulders in the mirror; his back turned to me to give me some illusion of privacy. He is lean and muscular. Still a boy, but you can just see the outline of a man's body. I remember with a stabbing sense of yearning for the chubby baby Burt was. My squishy little mellow bunch of pure baby goodness.

'And I need to do this before you leave.' The little shoulders are saying.

'Why?' I say, even though I know.

'Because Dad will never agree.'

There it is. The little shoulders expose the fear of a little boy being left by his mum for two weeks.

'That is not true. It depends on how you put it.'

'No, it does not; he always says no. To everything.' There is some truth in that, *in the No(m) of the Father,* Lacan said, but that won't be a helpful confirmation, so I go for something in the middle.

'That's not quite true, and nor is it fair.'

'It is true, and who cares if it is fair when it is true?' There it goes, the problematic truth-telling issue, but it will have to wait for another time.

Burt and Don have been clashing more than ever this past year. The obvious problem is they are too similar, but this is not a problem that is obvious to either of them. Neither like being told what to do, and never ever does either of them do what they are asked to do straightaway. There is always, always, a pause between the asking and the doing. The pause which seeks to insert autonomy. Something like 'I will do it in my own time.' Neither like being told they did something wrong. Both hate even more being told in public. Both react the same way. Which is to close down, walk off, refuse to talk, or shout. They are both deeply resentful of being impinged on in any of these ways while pretending things are "fine" and there is absolutely nothing to discuss. This is not how Hermione or I operate.

'He loves you, Burt. And he does things because he wants you to be a good person. With good values and a good approach to life. He wants you to be happy.'

'Bullshit. He does it because he has anger issues.'

Bullshit is Don's answer to many things I have said over the years. Things he doesn't want to hear.

'No. It is not bullshit, and he never used to have anger issues before we had children. What do you make of that?' I say as I realise, too late, this is not true, recalling a moment when Don threw a phone on the floor sending it to pieces once. He was angry at me. I can't remember what it was about, but I can remember leaving our flat and running away from it without knowing where I was going. Of course, I got lost. Very lost, and the run was much longer than I had in mind. It was dark when I eventually found myself back at the flat, relieved as much as I was surprised to see it when it appeared. The power of the unconscious drive.

'Are you saying it's my fault?'

'Nope. I am saying it is…

'My fault. If I wasn't born, he wouldn't have anger issues.'

'No. This is not a question of fault. I am saying that things don't happen in a vacuum. You know, like that lesson in chemistry, for all actions, there are reactions? One thing is a consequence of another. You do something, he gets angry, he shouts, you get angry, you do something, I shout and so on. A ripple effect.'

'Chemistry is not really your thing, Mum, and I think he just needs to stop shouting. You don't shout.'

'That's not true.' I am flabbergasted. I feel like I shout all the time.

'Not so quickly or so often as him. Anyway, back to my proposal, please?'

'I will need to talk to Dad first but it sounds reasonable to me.' I feel guilty for making Burt think Don wouldn't be angry if it wasn't for him. God, how stupid can I be sometimes, a big trampling elephant in the China shop.

'Ok. But I am telling you he won't agree.' With that, Burt walks out, content I have his back and content with himself for managing his expectations.

As Burt leaves my bathroom, I feel a sharp pang of sadness. Don finds it hard to hear but he is repeating something of his own early experience of being a son. Making Burt relive the feelings he had. He doesn't do it consciously. He doesn't mean to do it. That's when you deprive because you once were deprived yourself. It isn't that Don's father didn't love him. It is this memory he retains that his father wasn't there to watch him grow into a man, watch him grow to be good at things. That he didn't take an interest in things Don found fascinating. It is that he didn't watch his son play a game of rugby while being a coach to half the county. Don was desperate for his dad to see how good he was. But it didn't happen, and then he stopped being desperate and learned instead to not expect being watched at being good at something. And this was in danger of repeating.

There were no slaps, though. A different starting point. And I know Don loves Burt just like Don's father loves Don, which is to say, deeply and reliably. And that is good. But will good ever be enough for our children, I wonder.

CHAPTER 12
STILL TRYING TO FIGURE THINGS OUT

NEW ZEALAND, 2025

And things that happen when your father is a Rambo fan

I sit in my work armchair, askew like an S. My arthritis likes it. The arms of my work chair are worn by hours of arms leaning on them over the years, the colour fading in places, the silent witness to retold traumas. A black notebook waits patiently in my lap, pencil ready to collect the thoughts flapping around my head like a school of confused fish. I love a sharp pencil. The pencil loves moving on the smooth paper of the notebook; it's a new journey every time. The words start spilling out on the pages ruthlessly as I write my notes from a morning session that weighs on my mind more than it should.

I work from home now. I have a little self-contained unit away from our house, where I can go and be in a state of evenly suspended attention for my clients, uninterrupted by my private life, except perhaps my dogs. My client from this morning hates his father. At the age of twenty-eight, he is worried he will become like him. He hates his father and he fears his father and the two are connected. He hates him because he fears him. In the purse of human relationships, there are a few two-sided coins, two sides with seemingly opposing values that are, in fact, closely related and cost you the same. Hate and fear.

You fear what you hate, and you hate what you fear. Like a maggot inside a nice-looking cherry, you often can't see it, but it is eating at you, shaping you from the inside out.

I like old myths and legends. They mesmerise me with their lasting power. I often think of my clients' work as a mythological journey of discovery, similar to the ones I was told once upon a time, a hundred or so years ago. The ones where a hero sets out to see the world conquers some dark forces, wins a magic sword or a princess and returns victorious and wiser. The psychotherapeutic journey has more twists and turns, but it is where people come to learn about their dark forces and figure out their own magic sword. Because if they knew, they wouldn't need therapy.

Darius' first quest is to get past his Threshold Guardians. These take on different forms. For Darius, these Sphinxes go under the names of Hate and Fear. "Not nobody, not nohow" is their order. No one can get past them. He will have to be brave and look them in the face. He will have to get to know them, and he will have to make friends with them so that he can get past them. Some never will. Then he will have to face his arch nemesis, his Shame. She drives him to reject who he was born to be and pretend to be someone he isn't so that it looks like he is one of them.

I remember when he first sat in the chair opposite me two years ago, his hair impeccably restrained against its will, bursting under his hair paste, determined to be freed. Much like his body felt about the chair he was sitting in. I commented he looked like the chair was either too small or too big but just not the right fit for him. He smiled nervously and said, 'I feel like you can see straight through me.'

I stand up from my chair and walk towards the mirror hanging by the door, discreetly obscured by a plant with leaves trailing off the bookshelf next to it. I wish I could see through you, I say to my image, and it says it back, as if suffering from echolalia, even though it looks much too old.

It is funny how many people feel this. That that I can see through them. All these see-through people walking around the world, hiding lest they are seen and yet desperate to be known. Sometimes, I can, but that isn't what I am here to do. Not in my thinking chair. I am here to look at them, with them, not through them.

Darius is angry that his father won't say sorry. There is a list Darius has in his head of all the things he feels his father did to him. It will be a long time yet before Darius will realise that his father might have done all the things, but not *to* him. Darius worries he will become his father. He is often angry, like him, and he can't "do monogamous" no matter how hard he tries. Just like his father, he can't be alone. It's hard to be on your own when they are lurking in there. The Sphinxes. And you don't want to meet them.

Because he is harsh on himself, judging himself all the time, there is no fun in all the polygamy foxtrot that seems so promising to an outsider. It makes him feel good to berate his father in front of me. Berating is a form of loving that he has learned, and that is how he loves those close to him. Even if he might not do it out loud to all his girlfriends, it's there, and you feel it when someone judges you. It betrays itself in the small acts of unlove. Berating and judging is also how he loves himself, while telling himself he is just trying to fit in. But like Darius the Great, he will only ascend his throne and claim his own Self by overthrowing an imposter. In this Darius' case, the imposter is internal. The vagabond occupies him with a ferocity worthy of the emperor's name, but whom Darius paradoxically yet understandably came to call "the English people mentality".

Because of all the hate and fear that go on rampaging untethered inside him, reins firmly in the hands of the formidable Shame, that second in command to the imposter, Darius created this "personality" for himself, impersonating by the process of assimilation those he considers to hold all power. Thus, Darius went from one oppressive frying pan into another.

Darius' internal imposter and his unmet hate, fear and shame make me think of my own nemeses. I sigh; I have taken them on countless times over the years. I look back at my reflection in the mirror. I frown and now I can see him. I have his frown. What else?

Like my father, Darius thinks that scared means weak, and there is no place for weakness in the world where you can be killed if you are not strong. Forced once again to visit my own past fears, I remember how once, just like Darius now, I couldn't bear seeing vulnerability in myself or others. Like Darius, I was once scared of my father. I also hated him because I feared him, and I, too tried to be strong and never show it. Because if you show fear, the beasts will sense it. And they might devour you.

Shaking my head to dismiss the thoughts, I notice the stubbornly greying hairline in the mirror reflection. There is no getting away from it, but I am not yet ready to surrender. I don't feel grey yet, even if it frames me. Then I remember the other thing which no doubt plays a role in making Darius' problem feel more acute. It is the very present issue of my having to go and see my father. No one is making me, but something is making me, so I have to. Because another two-sided coin in the purse of human relationships is one with love and hate sides. I will have to traverse tens of thousands of kilometres in order to see him. And then, when I get there I will do anything to not see him. The terrible irony of it. And it's not just land and oceans that I will need to cross. Thousands of neural pathways that I will have to tiptoe, shimmy through, duck under, trying to find another way in and also out. Undo and redo. Every time. But there isn't enough time, really. At no time has there ever been enough time in one's lifetime to undo and redo certain kinds of wirings. Too many ruptures, increasing their indent, not enough repairs.

'Would you like some coffee?' the door opens with a bang, and Don walks in just as I jot down, *Who was my father. What kind of a man was he born to be.*

I put the pencil down and close my notebook, 'Yes, please'. I would love some coffee. Don has an uncanny ability to know when to interrupt. Me a rupture, he a repair. That's one of his superpowers.

'How was your morning,' Don asks as he passes the threshold of my evenly suspended thinking space, handing me the steaming cup of dark caffeinated goodness.

'Confusing.' I say as we walk out together into their garden where I can breathe out the session and taste the salt of the sea in the air, and hear the birds crack on with their songs. Everything outside is in such contrast to everything inside me. Like a flightless female firefly trapped in the lantern of a peaceful night.

Later that day, when the kids are in bed, and Don comes in, the bearer of comforting beverages bringing me a glass of wine this time, I pull the sheet up under my arms and return to my notes. *What did he want to be when he grew up? What kind of an idea of a man did he grow up with?*

'Do you think my dad planned to grow up to be an arsehole?' I say, with just enough ease to let Don know he is ok to go there. 'Like, the teacher said, hey Frank, what do you want to be when you grow up? An arsehole, Miss, yes, I think that is what I want to specialise in.'

Don puts my drink on the bedside table and walks around to his side of the bed. He slowly puts his cup down and says,

'Did he plan it? No, I don't think so. Did he want to? I doubt it. But he might have felt he had to. Also, I don't think he thinks he is an arsehole. He is what he had to be.'

'No.'

'No, what?

'I mean, yes, I agree with everything except the last bit.'

'He didn't have to be who he is?'

'Yes. And, no. He is what he *felt* he had to be. But bad things happen to people all the time. The thing that differentiates us is what we do when they do.'

'Yes, M. But he couldn't do anything else because if he could, he would.' Don says. I understand what he means. He is thinking logically. Frank, if he was a human machine, which is how Don approaches all things, dead or alive, was built that way. He wasn't given software to find a better solution to life. He did what he could with what he had at his internal disposal, which wasn't very much.

'He was too scared.' I say, after a while.

'Yes, and probably for good reasons.' Don says and opens his book on *How Things Work, The Universal Encyclopaedia of Machines*, Volume 2.

I pick up my phone to play a game of Solitaire. I remember that Darius' father played him all the *Rambo* films, before he was eight, before he smuggled him out of Syria for a better life. What did Darius think he was going to be when he grew up?

We shape humanity by the stories we tell our kids and by the stories we don't. By the clothes we put them in, the food we feed them or not. By virtues, we hold dear, by our prejudices, hopes and fears.

CHAPTER 13
SLOVAKIA, 2025

READY OR NOT, HERE WE COME

A short break that broke the camel's back

We are about to land. I hate landing, though not as much as I hate taking off, because getting closer to the ground feels less unnatural than getting away from it. Probably because I am not exactly a grounded person, I like to feel the ground under my feet. Contorted like a balloon animal, I am fumbling in my bag on the floor underneath the seat in front of me, sabotaged in my attempts by the seat belt, trying to fish out a small notebook to make a note of something. Most couples on the flight are a mixture of Slovakian and English, which, on the face of it, is unsurprising. The thing about the face of it is that you can always find something behind it. Something waiting to be found. It is a joy to hide but a disaster to not be found, as one child psychoanalyst said. The couples are made up exclusively of Slovakian women and English men. Not Slovakian men and English women. At all. Which is kind of curious.

Once, not that long ago, back on the Rock (as the locals fondly called their island), I spoke to a taxi driver taking me home after a night out. He was a Kiwi who went to the Philippines to get himself a wife, much in the same way that people go to India to get their teeth done cost-effectively. I was a bottle of fine red in, and I felt something unpleasant forming in the pit of my stomach as I heard the man say, "She is half my age, and her mother is *my* age." He laughed, so pleased with his fat self.

116

'That must be confusing,' I said dryly, but he either didn't hear the challenge, or he couldn't understand my accent with his colonial ear. His indifference to this malignant residue of all the wrong kinds of interventionism was so shocking I almost sobered up. Sadism was taking a walk down a fashion gangway, expecting applause.

However, I don't believe that Slovakian women leave their home country to find themselves an English husband to bring home like a great bargain you find at a flea market. It also isn't the case that they go off in search of a rich husband to woo and bring back. It is a long way to go for uncertain returns, and not many want to go back anyway. If it is a thing motivated by economic opportunities, there would also be Slovak men on this flight with English wives. But there weren't. It is about women seeking something which men don't. Something different to the prevailing insidious poverty of thought that was hanging over our country like a dark cloud.

So why do the women leave and the men not so much, I ask myself. Was it curiosity, courage or desperation that drove it?

I wonder if the men are prouder citizens; maybe they feel they have to stay. Maybe it is something about how men are brought up. Brought up to stay or return with the Holy Grail. Is that why my father stayed? Perhaps it means more to men to belong to a place that gave them life. A question of loyalty or honour. Or, maybe they just don't want to leave their mothers.

I have no convincing answers, and now the plane is screeching to a halt, to the seated ovation of its human cargo. Every time. I sigh inwardly. Every single time, I get irritated by this. Hermione says bemused, 'Why are they clapping Mum?'

Because they are a superstitious bunch of morons, I don't say.

'I think they are applauding the pilot.' I do say, neutrally enough, I hope.

'But he can't hear them,' says Hermione. Despite sounding like a statement, this is a question.

'No, he can't.' I confirm.

'So, why do they bother then?'

'Mum?'

'Hermione.'

'I said why do they bother then?'

'It might be a cultural thing. People from different cultures have different traditions and different ways of being and expressing themselves. Maybe they feel it is a nice thing to do, and maybe they also feel a bit relieved to have made it. They are not used to flying. As a nation, Slovakian people couldn't leave their country until 1995, so it is a relatively new thing for them to be able to fly.' But also, a lot of them are uneducated and superstitious, but I don't want to make my daughter as judgmental as I am so I keep this part of the sentence to myself.

Hermione is silent for a while and then says, 'But you are one of them, and you don't clap. You are not relieved to be here, are you?'

'Well, this is the problem with making generalisations. Maybe I am not one of them,' Hermione.

'What does that even mean?' I am irritated now with myself, with uneducated, superstitious people, and with Hermione too, 'Grab your bag, we need to get moving.'

'You are from *there*, so you are one of them, Mum. You never like it when I can tell the truth about something that you don't want to admit to me. Or sometimes to yourself, for that matter. I don't see why. I am your daughter.' Hermione fires back. Oh, that truth thing again!

Rescued by the aircraft door opening, we disembark and make our way to passport control. Even though a police uniform still has the power to make me feel like a criminal, I wish the queue was longer. I am not all that ready to face the other side.

As we walk towards the terminal's thin exit gates, I notice with mixed feelings how everything feels so worn about this country. The contrast between here and New Zealand couldn't be clearer. The cheap paint is peeling off in places, manual light switches in the toilets (which you are expected to switch off after use) are sticking to the wall, the plastic doors on the cubicles are lighter than your overhead luggage, and the sad rattle of the conveyor belt singing softly with its song, that it has never seen a better day; this country lets you know its story as soon as it lets you in, through the weakling creaky sliding doors.

I spot my mother in the small crowd gathered around the gate; she is smiling. She is so happy to see us. She makes her happiness depend on me and my children, which makes the smile almost unbearable.

'Father is waiting in the car near the airport. He finds it too much to walk bigger distances now and didn't want to pay for the car park,' she says apologetically, at the same time rolling her eyes and shrugging her shoulders, 'You know what he is like.'

Here we go, I think to myself. Here come the attacks veiled in conspiratorial off-handers, like it is something we share. But I smile and say I do. It will be a long four days.

The next day, the sun is out early and not stopped by the threadbare brown curtain that is supposed to block its entry. If you pull it too much to the left it won't cover the whole of the window on the right. I can hear the cuckoos singing a familiar tune, and it feels like they are the same ones that lived here when I was a girl. They don't live that long but their ancestors were here. How long have the cuckoos been singing their song, I wonder, a constant background to someone's life. Or, perhaps our lives are the background to the cuckoos' song; who is to say. I get out of my old bed and slowly walk up to the old, single-glaze window that Don would say could do with a lick of paint. I take in the scene that used to greet me every morning for many years. There is not much to see but the familiarity of it makes for something. The apple tree that I used to love climbing has shrunk. The apples under it are mostly rotten. The old bits and rusty bobs gathered into a corner- you wouldn't want a toddler or a small child running around there unsupervised.

The vegetable patch is tidy, and the rope still hangs off the cherry tree. The rope never quite made the upgrade to a swing. The cherry tree keeps its secrets. I shrug off the incoming thoughts and feelings which threaten to derail me, and I go to cuddle my daughter who is tucked up under a mele of sheets and bed covers. I can never get enough of that image, and it always has the power to stop me from thinking about anything else but Hermione's messy hair and warm red cheeks, which all say this is what a good night's sleep looks like.

The plan for today is that we are going to the cemetery. The three women, mothers and daughters, we will go and visit the oldest of my superheroes, who used to hide her superhero cape in her bottomless laundry basket.

It takes us a while to find it. A good sense of direction is not our thing. The grave is hidden in a sea of others, often separated by just enough of a path to fit only one pair of feet. They all have flowers and candles which are so plentiful they often obscure the name on the stone.

In the hot sun, the sweat on my Mum's face is confusing the tears; the three of us quietly swap stories of do you remember when, while tidying up grandma's last bed. The memory of the concrete being poured onto the coffin still produces a suffocating sensation, it tightens my chest and throat, and I can't breathe for a moment. It's as if a large dollop of cement was, by accident, deposited in the pit of my stomach and the weight of it makes me hold my breath. I could pass out. Pass out and sleep on grandma's lap once again. Being here feels dreamy. There is an otherworldliness emanating from the place and then Hermione makes us cry when she says this cemetery is sad and beautiful at the same time. 'It's sad people have to die,' she says, 'and there are so many people here that were once walking around here, like us now. But all these flowers, they are everywhere, Mum. They show you carry the dead ones in your heart. So they kind of never die, Mum, do they?'

There truly were so many colours in here. Each tombstone with its own lush little parcel of paradise. What an extraordinary thing for a country that is so poor to splash out on its dead. And they do. The shops selling all the cemetery paraphernalia are the best looking in town, with beautiful front windows, fresh paint and even air conditioning. What is wrong with this country, I wonder to myself, why do we value our dead more than our living? It's like the dead are rewarded for winning their life-long battle for triumphant melancholy.

My thoughts return to my Grandmother. As always, I am flooded with a sense of gratitude and sorrow. She was the best thing that could have happened to me. Without her, I would probably never have been able to learn to believe I was a good person and a person that someone could love. That I could love. Instead of constantly suspecting myself of some unknown badness.

Not bear me, put up with me, suffer my presence, make me feel bad or guilty, but actually treasure me, make me feel special and powerful and capable of big things. Even if I wasn't. For some reason, I remember the day I went into grandma's wardrobe. It required courage because the old mahogany piece was solemn as a priest, even if it was only kept shut by a folded piece of cardboard wedged between its doors.

With the greatest care, I extricated my grandmother's favourite shawl and put it around my neck ceremoniously, as if this threadbare cloth was woven with gold. Grandma wore it to keep her neck from getting cold. Women of her day protected their bodies from being entered by the cold through the gaps in their clothes. Head, necks and waistlines. They would wear these unsightly camisoles underneath their outdoor wear, tucked obsessively into their skirts. No trousers. Only skirts. Long enough to leave things to the imagination for sure, although I couldn't conceive of a place less likely to foster imagination than our murky old town. The shawl smelled like grandma, and it made me feel important and like a fully-fledged human being. I looked at myself in the three-way mirror and spoke to myself in a voice that belonged to a posh lady. *Good afternoon! How do you do?* Probably Ivana's mother. Kids always love playing adults.

Then the door opened, and Grandma walked in.

'Hello, young lady. That's a pretty shawl you got yourself there.' She said, slipping into the game seamlessly.

I beamed happily and then clarified, 'I am playing a dult, grandma.'

'A dolt? What is that, darling?' Grandma said, bemused.

'Silly Grandma. You know what a dult is! It is when people think that you can do things on your own, and they like you and have coffees with you and stuff. Oh, and you smoke, as well, if you want. You know, a dult. Like mum and dad and you and grandpa. When you are grown up all the way to how big you will grow.' I remember this because Grandma liked to tell this story and I heard it told many times. Grow up all the way to how big you will grow. I wonder.

Anyway, Grandma then scooped me up and told me in no uncertain terms that I would make the best adult there ever was in our family, and then she went and made us scones with my favourite homemade jam.

I had not thought about any of this for a long time. All that time wandering around the world, making and breaking myself and some boys' hearts, not believing my grandmother's words, not believing. I feel the tears at the back of my throat. I feel stupid talking to the stone but I do it anyway. I tell it things as if grandma is here, next to me. In some ways, she is. Who knows how we hear things when we die. Our ears may be dead, but the words still fall out of our mouths and float through the soil, into the cracks of the coffin until they lay down on what's left of our love. And it must at least touch. The words, like feathers in a soft down, falling onto her. How I miss her warm hands, sitting in her living room, watching her knit another pair of woollen socks, with that awful yellow wallpaper framing the scene, walls a witness to so many things, they go on standing while the scenes inside them change.

I am so sorry I didn't come more often, but also, why didn't Grandma call before she died. Why did she go dying alone. That was the worst thing for me to bear.

I am brought out of the corner of my memories with Hermione hugging me tight just above the waist, which is where she can reach. She doesn't say anything, she knows there are times when you don't. I wonder how my daughter knows these things as I blow my nose and straighten my back, taking Hermione by her hand. And then it is time to go.

As we walk back to the house, I wonder about the role of the men in this family. It is not a very good one. Grandma was buried on top of grandad, a question of space and chronology, not design. He was there too, and yet I gave him no thought, and I wonder why. What happened to our men? Why is there nothing good about them that wants to be remembered?

The three of us walk together in comfortable silence, interrupted occasionally by Hermione's thoughts. We walk across the town centre into a park with a pleasing shade and a small pond. Hermione is delighted to discover life in it, and the tadpoles are having a party. She gatecrashes it, and watching my daughter's face sparkle with joy, I feel my soul heal steadily, like a worm growing its cut-off tail. When we get home, my father says,

'Did you go and see your other grandparents?' He means his parents in the cemetery. Always on the lookout for something I didn't do right or did wrong, that's what it feels like.

I say yes; we put some flowers on both graves and tidied it all up a bit. There. Take that.

He shrugs his shoulders as if not really interested anymore.

'How are you, Dad?' I ask. This should be such an easy, ordinary question to ask, and yet it costs me so much.

'I live.'

'That doesn't sound like much,' I say, but what I mean is it doesn't sound like living to me.

'Life is not much for everyone.'

I can hear the low, threatening hum. I know the storm is impending.

'No. I guess it is what you make it.'

I can't help it. It comes out, and it gives me some satisfaction.

'You think you know everything, don't you?' And here it is. Raised eyebrows to match his voice, a deep burrow in the middle of his forehead. Some things stay exactly as you remember them, no matter the time. It didn't take long. Satisfaction is long gone; it feels threatening just like it used to, and I want to leave the room. I am scared but also full of rage. And I don't want to say something that will make us not speak for another five years.

'You think you are the smartest of 'em all, don't you?' he repeats the same accusation differently.

'What is it you think I should know and don't?' I ask quietly.

'You think because you could make things work for you, everyone else should be able to. No matter what.'

'Or is it that you think because you couldn't make things work for you, no one else should be able to?'

'You need to shut your mouth if you can't speak to your father with a bit of respect.'

'Oh, yes, respect. That's a good one, Dad. What about some respect for me, for once? Or, thanks for spending a fortune to come and see my father, who doesn't even speak to me unless it is to reprimand me? What about a sorry, maybe, for raising my hand to you, poking a knife at you for my amusement. What about any of that, Dad?

He is staring at me blankly, and it takes the wind out of that sail.

'And, still, I let you have a relationship with my children and my family when no one else can be bothered with you anymore. What about some respect for that, Dad?' I weaken now in my resolve. He seems so brittle.

He goes pale and sits down and I say, somewhat alarmed, 'Are you ok?

He mutters, 'Go, just get out of my sight.' His hand is shaking as he takes out a cigarette from his dirty overalls.

Hermione is around the corner and follows me to my room, saying, 'What happened, Mum? What were you talking about? Grandad looks terrible, and you look upset. What is it, Mum? What did he say? What did you say? What's wrong? Mum? Mum! Answers, please ?!'

'Not now, Hermione. Go and find Grandma. Give me ten minutes. Then I will tell you everything.'

'I am not leaving you.'

'Please. Just do as I ask. I need ten minutes.'

I gently usher Hermione out of my old bedroom and shut the door behind her.

'I am setting my alarm – ten minutes and not a second longer.' Hermione shouts through the door.

My heart is beating fast. I scramble around my handbag until I find the phone. I dial Don's number.

'Hello!' God, I love hearing him.

'I hate him,' I say.

Don says, 'How many times do you have to get hurt by that miserable prick before you realise you don't have to anymore?'

We avoid each other for the rest of the next day. It is the last day before we leave. Well, this visit worked a treat, I think to myself as I pack a bag for me and Hermione. We are going to the Lido. As we get in the car, he saunters up, shuffling his Parkinson's riddled feet and asks where we are going.

'Lido,' I say.

'Are you taking the car?' He asks, even though he can see we are taking the car. Here comes another ball as curved as his worn spine.

'Yes, is that ok?' Erecting an invisible fence around me, like Burt does on Fortnite, as fast as I can.

'Would have been nice to ask before you packed it.'

'Do you need it?'

'No, why would I need it, right? I don't need anything anymore, do I? No need to bother asking me, is there?' He looks so joyless and lifeless it tightens my throat in an unexpected emotion. He is right. I never thought to ask him because there is really no reason for him to be anywhere. There is no reason for him to be. But also, I have to admit this to myself- because I have that relationship with the truth, I also didn't ask because I knew he wanted to be asked. Could I really be this petty? This awful? This vindictive? Argh.

'Sorry. We can always get a taxi if you need it.'

'I know you can.' He walks off, defeated by life, and I feel dreadful.

How is this so difficult?

'Dad?'

'What?'

'We are only here for one more day. Do you want to come with us?'

'Are you mad? When was the last time you saw me going to the Lido, M?' but there is a trace of softness to his tone now. He appreciates the move I have made towards some kind of reconciliation. It isn't much, but that is all we are capable of.

When we left last time, two years ago, I felt awful for not giving him a hug. I had to soak a few tears in my sleeve, I didn't want the kids to see. They were not sold on leaving the hemisphere anyway, there was no point adding to it by seeing their mother distressed at the point of departure. I hugged everyone but him. We just never did that and now we didn't know how. I was determined the next time would be different.

It wasn't.

CHAPTER 14
COUNTRY ROADS, TAKE ME HOME

NEW ZEALAND, 2025

Leaving, homecoming and all that jazz

It felt like home — going back there, Mum, Hermione said when she came back from a horse-riding session recently. She hasn't been riding for a few months. She came off a horse who was spooked by the wind, and although she got back on, with time she started to feel more cautious and less safe. Caution sucks the joy out of things unless you are a scientist. She went back that time as we were looking for an activity for her during the school holiday. It felt like home being back, she said.

I feel a similar thing as our ferry draws closer to the terminal of our little island. It feels like home being back here. I could fit the island in between my arms from this perspective. Like those people on holidays who take pictures of holding up the Eiffel Tower, or the Leaning Tower of Pisa. A trick of the eye. Looking at it from this distance, it feels like home. I am not sure if that's an illusion, too, but this feeling in my chest feels real enough. Even though I don't obsessively seek to name it, it feels good to be back amongst the lush green growth surrounded by the pretty sea. People, not too many, but always a friendly face somewhere, mostly nothing is ever too much trouble for anyone. It is a parallel universe to the one I occupy internally where most things are potential trouble. Walking to the car park, I spot Nieve from the corner of my eye. Nieve is a local dog groomer. She interviews the dogs she grooms. I am hoping Hermione doesn't spot Nieve as I don't feel like talking, and Hermione doesn't understand what that is like. Having to talk right now would be like walking into a wall you didn't know was there while trying to find a toilet in the middle of the night.

Neive's dog interview is a rigorous process. She insists on a home visit, too, to see what the dogs are like in their own environment. Their owners, too, no doubt. I have always thought that owners of dogs and the dogs of their owners are intrinsically linked in character and, more subtly, in looks. My dog is an exception to the rule. Pooch is friendly and happy. Everyone loves Pooch, and she loves everyone. Most of all, Pooch loves me. Not everyone loves me, and I am not always friendly or happy. I also can't get over how little a dog wants in exchange for how much they give.

Some people make fun of the selective dog grooming services, but I understand. It's like when therapists say between themselves, "I am only taking on nice neurotics these days, no more BPDs for me." I hate labels for things because I think they deny things the opportunity to speak for themselves. Also, the "BPD" label has become chronically overused, misused and misunderstood. Borderline Personality Disorder. The border is meant to be the one that divides the neurotics from psychotics, so the "BPD patients" are a bit of both. I am sure everyone is on this spectrum in some way, on some days, to some extent. One of my clients keeps throwing it at herself all the time during her sessions, the label a curtain to hide behind or a whip to beat her herself with. She fell out with her father when he commented on her appearance one day, harshly, cutting to the quick. Unwittingly, she replaced her father with the label. They both functioned to make her feel dysfunctional and inadequate, like an ugly duck in the world of swans, doomed for eternity to be defensive. BPD definition contains over two hundred characteristics, which basically includes the entirety of the female experience during any hormonal changes. It is sexist, it is misogynistic, as well as it is inadequate. But I digress. I understand why Nieve would not want to have a BPD dog for a client. And, of course, Pooch passed the interview with flying colours. Pooch has no personality disorder of any kind. She is a lovely neurotic, absolutely clear in her purpose in life. An eternal people-pleaser, she is here to make everyone that bit happier.

Driving home, windows down, John Denver going up and down his country road, I am relieved to be back. Hermione is excited despite the jetlag. Her head is sticking out of the window, hand outstretched, and she yells a loud 'Hii' and 'Nice to see you again, Moira,' to the lady who sells the handmade cushion covers at the local Saturday market. Moira's hand raises in return with a wave and a smile. I smile because it is a funny thing my daughter has come to love life in a small town.

'Mum?'

'Here.'

'Why doesn't that guy have a wife? Adding, 'Or a boyfriend or something?'

She heard me correct myself like this in a conversation recently. Naturally, she had to try it out.

'I don't suppose you could be a bit more specific?' Looking around outside to see if there is anyone matching the description that only exists in Hermione's head but which she feels confident her mother will intuit.

'The old guy who comes for a cup of tea? Uninvited?'

'Duggie. I wouldn't call him old, exactly. And you don't always need an invite for a cup of tea. It is a nice thing to do, to call in on someone, unexpectedly. It shows you think about them.' I say, utterly unconvinced about the truth of my statement.

'Yes, him. Why?' Half-satisfied we are getting somewhere.

'Well, he is not that old…'

'Mum!'

'He had one, and they got divorced.'

'Why?'

'I don't actually know exactly.'

'Why do people get divorced generally, Mum?'

'I don't think there is a general reason, but I suppose if there was, it would be that people grow apart.'

'What does that mean? Grow apart. It sounds like they were one thing, and then they grew into two things. Like a road that forks into two at the bottom of our driveway?'

'Good question.' I say, 'although I don't like it one bit, because I already know I am going to overexplain. Also, I think that is much more a Burt question than a Hermione one.'

'Well, I think it's more so what they had between them, something they created together that can become thinned out like that fork in the road. I think we could call it a "relationship". Two people cherish it as one until one day, one of them starts to cherish it less, and it starts to weaken. It no longer has all it needs to keep strong because it is being pulled into different directions.'

'So Duggie's relationship fell apart. Like a house of cards. Not grew apart.'

'Yes, Hermione, something like that. But it probably happened over a course of time, rather than suddenly – like a house of cards might.' I say, finicky as fuck. I have no idea why I can't just let it be imperfect. No one cares. Except for me. I can't believe when I hear myself add, 'Maybe it is that people *grow away* from each other. Which you sometimes refer to as growing apart.'

'But why, Mum?'

'Why what?'

'Why did one of them start to cherish it less?'

'Because to start with, they thought they wanted one thing, but as they grew older, they realised they wanted something different. Either all along, or it changed over time.'

'I see. Like me with hummus. I used to think I liked it for a long time, but I don't anymore.'

'Yes, you grew out of liking it.' I reply, agreeing, while also thinking how hummus and humans sounds similar. Best not get stuck on that.

'Mum, can you grow out of love?'

'Yes and no, I think. But you might still have love and grow apart.'

Hermione goes silent, and I ask myself why I can't just give a simple, age-appropriate answer. Maybe I don't know it myself. My own parents should have grown apart, but instead, they just didn't grow at all, and they did it together, which makes me think of my next bright idea.

'Did you know there is this thing called epiphyte?'

'No, what is that? And what has it to do with people getting divorced?' Hermione says, slightly weary now.

I am not sure yet. I think maybe it has to do with people *not* getting divorced when they should. 'It is a living thing with no roots. A plant that grows on another plant, usually tree trunks, in tropical rainforests. They are here on the island.'

'What has that to do with people getting divorced, Mum? Are you saying his wife grew on Duggie, and then one day, because she had no roots, she took off and went to live on another trunk? And you still haven't really explained why. That is the question. There are so many people in my class who are divorced. Sometimes that worries Burt,' she says, letting it trail. And I know it does, but until now I didn't realise it also worried Hermione. So, I won't say to Hermione that the big epiphytes are called widow-makers. If they fall from the tree, they can kill anyone below, as broken marriages can, too.

'It's just a metaphor, Hermione.' Probably not the best one, I think to myself, but I never let that deter my metaphors. I continue, 'Which means that one thing can stand for another thing. Like when you made that erupting volcano sculpture for the school project to represent our family - remember?' I decide to ignore the worry for the moment.

'Which, by the way, I still don't quite understand...' I don't get to finish my attempt at distraction.

'...oh yeah,' Hermione hides her one-side smile at the memory, she knows what she meant with her sculpture. 'Like a symbol, right?' She says, pleased with cementing her learning.

'Yes, exactly like that. So what I was thinking is that these epiphytes living on trees are a little bit like people who fall in love. They find each other and share their lives as one, even though they are two separate beings. They like the same things, and these things feed them.'

'Ok, I get that. But why come apart? Wouldn't staying together make them stronger and live longer?'

'Well, I think it can, but maybe it can also do the opposite. So it can do both things, make them thrive or make them suffer if they become incompatible.'

'Mum.'

'Incompatible?'

'Yes.'

'It's like mismatched, like the wrong half in the pairing cards game. So they become unable to be a pair.'

'Mum.'

'Still here.' I don't think I like the tone of that.

'Why wouldn't you just give me a normal person answer like he found himself a new girlfriend? Or she found herself a new boyfriend. Or they kept on being angry with each other because of their kids, and in the end, they just had enough of everyone always shouting, and they decided to leave. No cards, no roads, no trees, no trunks, no plants, no falling, no growing apart. Just people getting sick of each other. Like you and Dad.' There is a tremble in her voice, and I feel terrible.

'Hermie?'

'Yes?'

'Dad and I are not falling apart. We are growing together. He has not found himself a girlfriend, and I have not found myself a boyfriend. And no one is leaving.' Yet, I don't say. It's no time for bad jokes.

'Ok. You better not be lying, Mum. Or using some meterfor that I am not getting.'

'I am all metaphored out. Shall we get some ice cream?'

Ice cream is magic. It lights up little girls' eyes.

When we get home, Don and Burt are there, waiting for us. Walking into the lit house from the car, it looks like one of those homes you steal a glimpse into, from the cold and dark outside, and inside, it's Christmas. Those houses that look like a home. I have one of those now. A home. My home. I put the suitcases down and remembers a line from Bob Dylan's song, *"I have been in trouble ever since I put my suitcase down"*. But this trouble feels life-affirming. Burt says thank god you are back, Mum, and he comes into my arms for a hug. He is getting so tall.

'Nice to see you too, Burtie. Say hi to your sister.' I say as I reluctantly let go of him. He let me hold him for a bit longer than usual.

'H' is as much as Burt is prepared to get out in the vague direction of his sister.

'I got you a present,' Hermione says, mischief in her eyes.

'Oh yeah?' Burt feigning disinterest.

'Yeah,' question mark on her face, 'so, are you going to say hi properly?'

'Hi,' he says this time.

'Oh no, that's not properly. You have to let me have a hug.'

'No way.' And then, 'What's the present?'

'You know what you have to do,' she says, expectant. She knows his need to have things will prevail, and the hug will come.

The way this works is that Burt will, in the end, let Hermione give him a hug. He is twelve, and hugs for his sister are out of the question in the universe of Eminem's Godzilla. The universe where he will argue that milk is black if he is in that mood, and where "no" or "it wasn't me" is his default answer. Also, "You are sexist", and "you always take her side", and "See? You love her more than me". Burt has expectations of me that he doesn't have of Don. Burt says it's because Don always says no, so what's the point? I wonder how many times in the last two weeks Don said yes because Burt lets Don put his arm around him as they sit down to eat together, and also he smiles at Don's jokes, however reluctantly and however Dad the jokes are.

We play cards later, and then I have a bath. I lock the door and close my eyes to inhale the lavender and exhale all the carbon dioxide from the air I breathed in while in the country of my birth.

In the morning, we decide to go to the Saturday market. The sun is shining, and people are smiling, not remembering the bad things today, and there is a good coffee smell shimming about between the stalls, which displays all kinds of things a person can make or imagine.

'Mum?' says Hermione, and not waiting for an answer, 'Can I have five bucks?

'And not a penny more.' I say.

'It's a cent, Mum.' Hermione corrects me. 'We haven't lived in penny-land for over a year now. When are you going to get used to it?'

'I am quite used to it, I think, Hermione.' I say, wondering how satisfying it is to obdurately hang on to things. That way, they stay alive. You keep them that way.

'Oh yeah, so why do you still use the water for the wipers on the front window instead of the full beam headlights when you are trying to say thank you to another driver?' Hermione accuses.

Ok, that one is less satisfying, I think to myself, only managing an 'Err…' before I am cut off by my daughter, who still only comes up to below my shoulder but who is beginning to be a sizeable match in obduracy.

'And instead of indicating to the left you put the wipers on?' Hermione continues with the Indictment of all the charges appertaining to my "Not getting used to living in the now".

'Here is five bucks, Hermione, don't spend it all on the lollies. Off you go now.'

'Love you, Mother, you are the best,' a quick squeeze around my waistline that makes my kidneys cry out loud and Hermione is off. She can see a friend in the distance and is running through the market's helter-skelter, like a spry feline on Paris rooftops. I look until I can't see her anymore, taking a picture in my mind, of this hopping skipping girl that looked so much like me as a girl, and thought it was the best thing ever.

I sit down on a wooden bench on the outside ring of the market. I am with Don, and we sit, people-watching. The caramel slice stops us from talking until there is nothing left but a taste for more, which can never be satisfied. Watching them milling around, I think about this island's people. It takes a certain type of person to want to live on a small island, and every day, I like it a little bit more than I did the day before. And, although there is always the sour taste of exception to the sweetness of the rule, it's easy to avoid it. You just look away. We humans have plenty of practice in that. Those who don't fit your idea of a human don't want to talk to you anyway.

The island is both small enough and large enough. It is small enough to bring a community together and large enough not to feel embraced too tightly or for too long. There are those who oppose looking out to the world because "we have our own problems."

Like the bike lane, which is not wide enough. Or the bike lane, which is not long enough. Or, just the bike lane. Or, what's worse – the horse poop or the dog poop on the beautiful beaches we have frequented for the last thirty years before *everyone else* came here. Even if they were *everyone else* themselves not that long ago. Or those who write to the local paper to illuminate their lifelong struggle with street numbering. You just put your head down when you see them. You can hear them a mile away.

The island is also not too far from and not too close to the mainland. Not too close to too many people and their multitudinous neuroses, but not so far that you forget what it is like to be neurotic. Not too far from culture and interesting world cuisine but not too close, so you get burnt by a flash of fire from a frying pan that is too many people living in one place too close to each other.

I spot Constance in the crowd, queuing, probably for the cheese bread sticks and the cinnamon brioche. For some reason, I remember our first conversation at the local Hall. I remember how things can go from good to bad so fast and so imperceptibly. How we can suddenly find ourselves at the edge of the reason, pulled by our emotions left or right never the centre, this edge we need to traverse carefully, or you fall over to the other side, when you become utterly othered. At one point during that first evening we met, I asked Constance if she worried about the effects of moving around the world when her boy was little.

'No. Did you?' A quick look unequivocally asking *are you judging me*, while at the same time, it felt to me like an attack. *You are doing the same thing, remember?*

'Absolutely. I worry about that kind of thing a lot. Still do them, though.' I said, friendly but braced.

'Oh. You do? Why?'

'Well, it's the way of things, isn't? Larkin said, *they fuck you up, your mum and dad, they may not mean to, but they do.* You know, if it's not one thing, it's your mother and all that?'

Constance laughed and drank some wine, 'I haven't heard that before.'

We navigated the edge successfully.

When Don came outside to join us for a cigarette that evening, I felt slightly dizzy with delight from the heights I had just traversed in that conversation and probably all the wine I drank. I told Don to meet my latest best friend. Don laughed, and Constance smiled.

Constance and I were daughters of different men. Two daughters two fathers, we all had different legacies to bear. And, we all four were children of places in the world burdened by different histories. All of us subjugated by a different past.

When Constance sees us, we wave, and she brings the swirls and sticks, and we make room for her on the bench.

'Isn't it a lovely day?' Don says.

CHAPTER 15
ONETANGI BEACH

2025

The weeping sands.

I am walking the dogs on a beach called The Weeping Sands. Onetangi. It comes from a battle in 1821 during the Musket Wars, which saw a series of thousands of battles and raids fought throughout the country among Māori from 1806 to 1845. These were intertribal arms races to gain territory or seek revenge for the past hurts. The death toll was unprecedented, with some 40,000 losing their lives. The sands would weep indeed. Lost in thought, I pick up a handful of sand and let it fall slowly through my fingers. For some reason, the sand makes me think of snow. Sand that soaked up the blood and covered the mess in the way that snow does, falling fresh all over the countryside. This makes me remember another moment in my life when I picked up a handful of snow in my hand from a bench next to me. It didn't fall through my fingers. The snow was sticky and creaky in that snow-way it has.

It wasn't too long after I moved to Prague that I found myself sitting on a snow-sodden bench at the City's Main Square. It was late, and it was cold. A thought of my grandmother came as if to warm me up, and with it, a memory of us reading together Hans Christian Andersen's *Little Match Girl*. As if in some twisted *I told you so,* my gaze tripped over and stopped at the top of the square, where there was a bronze equestrian sculpture of a saint on his fine-looking high horse, holding a pike, victorious. The whole thing sitting on a pedestal of polished granite, high, towering above the ants-people milling around in the after-work rush, I felt a jolt of young person's anger with the indifference of the statue to the world around me. This Leader of the Czech Lands, "our Prince". "*Do not let us die nor those yet to come*", it said on the sign under it. The Czech Republic was declared independent in front of the statue in 1918. Well, so much for that. Like the country, I was finding independence came at a cost.

I had just left Peter and was homeless. I was made homeless because my new roommate, with whom I was about to rent a flat, did a runner. She was an older woman; she felt old at the time, but she couldn't have been more than forty-five. She was divorced and apparently a thief. She was Slovakian, like me, and she tricked me into a sense of security when she suggested we rent a flat together so that I wouldn't have to live in a student hostel anymore. Seemed attractive. This was despite the fact that I once woke to find the woman staring at me with a knife in her hand. The woman was staying temporarily in the hostel with me, on the pretence she was my mother visiting. She was in some kind of trouble, and I felt sorry for her.

Anyway, the woman did a runner with my rent money, and the landlord threw us out before our suitcases could make an acquaintance with the floor. For some strange reason, I remember the brown leather of the suitcase, with two belts at the side to close it up with. With the suitcase came a man I had dated briefly when I first arrived in Prague; I can't even remember his name. How terrible, I thought. He gave me the suitcase as a goodbye present. The suitcase man. He had no need for it anymore. He found a place he wanted to stay. Lucky him.

And I found myself on a bench, homeless. It was late, and it was snowing that night.

But things always happen when you think, 'Fuck. What now.'

Not always good things.

A girl with too much makeup approached me and asked for a cigarette, which was the one thing I could still say I rightfully owned at this point.

'Sure.' I said as I opened up the yellow packet of Camels, holding it out for the girl to help herself.

'You right?' The girl asked.

'Not exactly,' I said, staring ahead.

'What's up?' I could feel the girl was curiously studying me from the side.

'Don't have anywhere to stay tonight.'

'Oh. Can I?' The girl motioned at the bench I was sitting on.

'Sure.'

We sat in silence for a while, with our shapes imprinted in the snow on the bench, staring in front of us. What we saw was people walking up and down and around, milling around like giant ants, looking directionless but all-knowing where the nest was. Unlike us. It's as if no one bothered to tell me and this girl. I looked at her from the side, wondering which one of us was more fucked up.

'You could come with me. But you are probably not going to like it.' She said seeing something in me she didn't see in herself, nor I in myself, either.

I was figuring things out fast. The girl must be a prostitute.

'Where to?'

'Just round the corner. It's a flat in Old Town Square. It's a nice flat. Good location, too.' She said, bitter-sweet.

'How much does it cost?'

'Oh, not much.' She said, turning to look away from me, adding, 'We could have fun, you know? The owner cooks really well.'

I thought it sounded like a strange arrangement but I didn't have many choices because I had no money and I couldn't ask my employer for another advance. I had only been there two weeks. They would probably let me go if I did, and now was not the time to be a jobseeker.

'Alright,' I said. What did I have to lose.

Turned out I had a bit to lose. A bit of myself, anyway. I hadn't understood it early enough. I was smart, but I was naïve. And I was reckless with myself. I didn't think I was that precious. Nasim let me stay. I had my own room, and he did cook good food for us all to share. The flat was occupied by a number of young Arabic men. We would all eat together in a circle on the floor, laid with a beautifully woven tablecloth. Looking back, it was as if I was conducting an experiment in which I was only partially present. The other part of me was hovering, watching from above. The men didn't speak my language, and they didn't speak much at all except for Nasim and his second-in-command. Nasim came for his payment one night. I had been there for about two weeks. I said, 'What the fuck are you doing?' and 'No fucking way', once it became clear. He stopped what he was doing while holding me down and said, 'Did you really think this was all for free.' And I said, 'No. I thought I was going to pay you in money, you prick.' Then he went back to what he was doing. He tried, and I fought. He tried hard. I fought, but in the end, I gave up. It didn't take long after that.

I learned two things that night. One, this was how some men still thought in the 20th century, and two, once a man was on top of you, there was no chance of you fighting them off. I was lucky they didn't try to do anything worse. When he finished, I got up, had a shower, packed the brown leather suitcase and left. It was a quarter past midnight.

I remember now, too, it was this memory that came to me that night in Prague when I was lying in the hospital bed after the botched abortion, and it made me feel sick. I didn't let myself get in touch with the whole of the pain then because it was too much. All I kept thinking then was why did I keep on putting myself on the cliff edge time and again.

That night, when I left Nasim's, I bumped into Daniel on my way to Café Rouge. He used to come to the café I worked in on Thursdays for a drink and a conversation. His newspaper office was above the café. Daniel was a good man. He was mad, but he had principles. He offered me a room in his flat temporarily, expecting nothing in return. Because, some days, life is like that. Truly dark but with a light always flickering somewhere in the distance.

I take my shoes off to feel the warm sand on my feet, and something drops on my hand as I bend down. I find that on my face, there are tears, and there are more of them in my eyes, and they all want to get out. It took them twenty-five years. A sob comes all the way from my gut like a howl of a wolf at the moon as I let the shame transform into pain, and then I take a deep breath, straighten up and walk on. If anyone I know walks by, they will just think it was the wind that blew some sand in my eyes, making them water. They were the Weeping Sands, after all.

CHAPTER 16
I AM STILL DISCOVERING THE ENTIRE TRUTH

NEW ZEALAND, 2025

On the edge of reason

I am cleaning the kitchen. Don is doing the lawns. Constance and Elliot are coming over later. I have a sensible relationship with my kitchen these days based on mutual respect. When Don and I were first elevated to the position of Having a Kitchen of our own, I would use it and clean it every night. My kitchen was my baby. It felt dizzyingly grown up to chop onions and peel garlic, and to put things away after. To wipe the counter, scrub it clean, and put everything to rest overnight in its designated place. It would look shiny, just like those images on the cleaning products I used.

It is a fact that a tidy and clean kitchen creates a powerful illusion of being in control of your life. So, once we had kids, my relationship with the kitchen changed. Like a mirror, it accurately reflected my life, which was mostly a smudged mess. The old "baby" went on to suffer separation anxiety and neglect, probably up until the point the children reached the age of seven or so. I found space in my head to make space in my life once again for my old friend, the kitchen. I am not a great cook, to put it mildly, and my kids are not great eaters, and I don't know which came first. As they never appreciated my more solid attempts at cooking, I resorted to the minimal standard of food preparation.

These days, I clean my kitchen when I feel like it. As I never clean it when I don't feel like it, there will be evenings when I go to bed, and the kitchen will not be cleared or cleaned. Unimaginable stuff for Don's or my mother. The kitchen doesn't mind, though, and it never takes too long before I need that illusion of being in control of my life just a tiny bit. It's the same with the fridge. Don likes things under control, which means he would probably like the kitchen to look more like a show kitchen as our garage does, but it is not often he makes this into my problem. And I treat our garage as his space.

I am scrubbing the surface of the white counter; why does it have to be white, which is also porous, just like my mind these days. The red wine that somehow always gets to the bottom of the glass to leave a ring of memory on the surface it touches and coffee stains from my careless pouring are stubborn like dried Weetabix in yesterday's breakfast bowl. I am thinking about Constance. There has been something on my mind since Constance's recent visit. It was a Sunday a couple of weeks ago, and Constance came with her dad. We talked that day long after the sun went peering from behind the horizon to give us some privacy. Some things just don't want to see the light of day. They can't be seen in full glare because the detail is too much for your eyes. Me, Constance and her dad talked that evening about things that were important to us from our own different perspectives. It was a knot we have been trying to untangle for a long time now, but all you do is pull out a few threads, get frustrated, put it down and go back to it later. Over and over. That Sunday, we had quite a lot of help from the old master, the almighty red wine and as always in such company, you think you are onto something.

I can't stop thinking about this feeling that has lingered over me since their visit, a feeling I can't find the right name for, this sense of *question* about how close Constance and her dad are. I feel a sense of both admiration and profound envy at his ability to find words to show her how sorry he is for the mistakes he made. A deep respect for his courage to be vulnerable in showing how much he needs Constance's forgiveness. How he asks for it time and again, even in front of me, and it doesn't emasculate him or make him seem weak. But also this. The un-answerability of this question: how did Constance disappear the hurt her father caused? I know for a fact that she carried it with her like a favourite soft toy, hidden out of view, for most of her life. Because I can see it with my own eyes and I hear it with my soul, she disappeared it like a clever magician. Unquestionably and unequivocally, it seems. And I am left with this feeling for which I can't find a name. And it is eating me up. Surprise, awe, envy, defeat, all at once.

Don pokes his head in through the ranch sliders; 'could you pass me a glass of water? It's bloody hot.'

I pass him the water and ask if he has forgiven his father for not always being the father he wanted him to be.

'Yes, I guess. No point in not. It won't change anything.'

'Why not tell him how you feel though? Or felt. It might make you feel better. Telling him. It will give him a chance to say sorry.'

'I don't think so. I thought about it. I think he is sorry, so all it will do is make him feel worse,' Don says slowly and thoughtfully as if it is a little mechanical discrepancy of living life which has to be overlooked because it can't be fixed. The machine is still in good working condition.

So there it is. Don could disappear hurt, too. Like Constance.

'Yes,' I say, 'it would do that. And that won't make you feel better, will it?'

'No, M, I don't think it would,' he says as he passes me the empty glass and kisses me before he disappears into the garden.

That night when we first met, Constance shared with me her deeply, singularly private thing that was fragile like a Christmas bauble, composed of shame, hurt, humiliation, anger and difficulty to forgive. I was intrigued. I was intrigued by this private woman who just shared a shocking and painful secret with me — almost a stranger. It seemed that Constance, like me, when I reveal intimate details of my life to almost strangers, was not seeking an audience who would feel sorry for her. She didn't care for people's pity or sympathy. Sometimes, you share painful things because it feels good. It is a relief to be heard by a person who you somehow know understands pain. Once it's out there, between the two people who know pain, it loses some of its power to hurt. But also Constance was always open to another way of seeing things. Always on the lookout for a new perspective, for the best pitch or formulation of the painful conundrum that was her way of coming to terms with her husband breaking the most precious bauble in their collection. It went by the name of Trust. You need many times to come to terms with some things because once is not enough. It doesn't have the power to last forever. Constance was looking for another layer of healing because the current one was leaking at times. The thing that I sensed that night but didn't know until this moment in my kitchen scrubbing away at things was that Constance may help me find another way of seeing some things, too. Things about forgiveness.

Filling up the kettle to make some more coffee, I feel on my way to some new realisation. When you are let down by someone you are supposed to be able to trust, it is a stab in the gut that you don't expect because they stab you while looking you lovingly in the eye. Not expecting is a big part of the hurt. It disorientates you, as though you are an infant all over again, not understanding anything around you because the things you thought you knew just became undone. However, I think as I wipe the sweat droplets off my forehead, God, it's hot; it is probably a better evil if you once knew how to trust than where your baseline is that you must not trust anyone. Especially not those closest to you. Because then, before you can learn anything new, you will first have to unlearn the deeply entrenched foundations of your own school of life of How and Why Never To Trust Anyone. And this is the difference between Constance and me. Constance, like Don, trusts in goodness in people. That is their baseline.

Three and a half scoops of black ground coffee go into the coffee plunger. I need to take five, and it smells good but it is not distracting the flow of my thoughts. I am on the home straight, even though I don't know what's at the end of this run. I can feel it. When I sat down with Constance for the first time, it was cold and we had to wear coats to be able to stay outside to smoke and be away from the other people. We both found big groups either over or underwhelming. We didn't care about the cold or if people thought we were rude. It was an important first meeting of our minds, which had to be allowed to take its course. I knew, in my gut, my soul, and before I could possibly know on a conscious level, that Constance was an unwrapped gift. A gift from the randomness of the universe.

When one mind correctly senses that another mind is willing and ready to hear some things, the mind facilitates the mouth with the articulacy it didn't know it had. Words come and go out of one mind into another, and then there is a new space opening in the original mind, which is ready to receive something back, modulated by the other mind. It becomes a little less heavy. Only a fraction, but fractions can tip the scales. To let yourself be held in another's mind like this is the thing which has the potential to begin to heal the cracks in your soul. You know the moment when it arrives. It feels like a warm sun on your face, even if it's cold and dark outside and all you can taste is the smoke of your last Marlborough light.

Constance said that night, I worry sometimes when he goes away. What if, you know, it's there? At the back. After a short pause, I pointed out that he didn't break the bauble when he was away. He did it at home. It was as if he wanted her to find out. Some things seem at first too absurd to say out loud, but they are still a thing. Constance said she never thought of it like that. There was some relief in her voice, but I wasn't sure if she was just being polite. Surely, she must have thought of that.

But I wanted to understand one thing very acutely.

'How do you come back from that?' I asked Constance that night. After a while, in which we were both lost in thoughts about the men who abused our trust, Constance said, I don't know if you do.

Coffee brewed and poured, it has that lovely tiny bit of foam on the top, making it look smooth and delicious. I remember thinking that night, how do you come back to a place of trust once you have been shoved down a dirty alley of betrayal. Why would you go back to it knowing it had this back door that could be opened to let the wolves in. You should probably look for a new place to find trust. A safer place. But now, a new thought occurs to me. It might seem safer to leave but maybe then you end up on the move all your life. I gasp silently and then take a sip of my burning hot coffee.

Back that night, feeling like I hijacked the conversation in my mind at least, I said 'I think that sometimes people do bad things hoping to be found out.'

'But why would they want that?' Constance asked.

'Because once the secret is out, the wait is over. Once it's revealed, it becomes a test of the other's love. It becomes someone else's problem. Pass it like it's hot.'

'But why would you do that when everything feels so good? Why would you jeopardise losing a good thing? For what?'

Because you don't think ahead. Because the moment feels too good. Because you hope not to be found out, or you hope to be forgiven. Maybe, because you are being true to yourself. Ruthless, but true. You want to find out who you really are. What you really want. And sometimes, you can't find out any other way than by hurting someone else. But I think something small gets killed in the act of forgiveness. A little girl's or a little boy's dream of a happy ever after. An idea of how life should be. Still, if you are lucky, something new may be born out of it.

Obviously, I didn't say any of these things to Constance that night, partly because I had no idea why Elliot himself would have done that, and also, it seemed wrong to guess at things when someone's hurt is an open wound. You don't jab it with some potion, hoping for the best.

'I don't know,' I said instead, 'but it seems to happen quite a lot that people who do a bad thing and are found out are with people who forgive them.'

'Why?' Constance asked, looking at me like I might have an answer.

I said I didn't know. I was not a forgiving type. But now I see the sad truth of it clear as day, doing a dance in front of me. By not forgiving him, I have denied my father an opportunity to do better by me. I have denied it to myself, too. I wouldn't let him feel better not allowing for a possibility of something new to emerge. A new relationship where he would feel forgiven and I would feel loved. What a fucking tragedy. By not forgiving him, I was being just like him. Cruel and punishing. Denying him a chance to be loved by his only daughter. Why do that?

The kitchen is nearly done. Only the cooker is left to do. Watching the grease on the stove dissolve under the chemical attack of a goo from a pretty-looking cleaning container. I am trying to find out the answer to my own question, which only turns out to be two more questions. Why is it that some people can forgive a thing that is hard to forgive? How do they do it?

Soaking up the grease in the kitchen paper towel to save the drain, I find the two questions have babies. Is betrayal of trust the worst thing that one human can do to another? When is betrayal a betrayal? I am back and forth in my mind, thinking about Constance and me, our respective points of hurt. They are different but they are the same too. Hurt is a hurt.

The implied or explicit promise of unbreakable trust inherent in certain relationships is considered sacred for good reasons. Individual people, like societies, need something to organise themselves around. Otherwise, incest and murder would be ripe, and we would live in darkness. But there are many reasons which can make a good person do the wrong thing. People never do something (wrong) without there being a reason behind it. Breaking the rule of trust, which underlies the basic structure of a human relationship, is not an easy thing to do. You have to be driven by something stronger than your love for the person and your otherwise general adherence to the rules of your culture when you set out to break them. Some demon you don't know resides in you and can control you. Something unresolved, asking to be brought to the surface. Like the grease on my stove.

The truth is flitting about like a small bird trapped inside a dwelling. It is not sure if it wants to be let out. It also seems too simple or too naïve. Like an ordinary act of human kindness. Just an ordinary act of human kindness, which requires Godly strength to gingerly traverse the abyss left after the betrayal and a profound understanding of human nature and its idiosyncrasies. An ordinary act with vast ramifications that probably ensures we survive as a species. But does everyone deserve a second chance?

More questions. It's always just more questions. The stove is done, and the kitchen looks like a young girl ready to stride out on Friday night.

I sit down in my new-looking kitchen, pulling a chair out for my feet. One more cup of coffee before I go get ready for the evening. It will take much less time and effort than it did to spruce up the kitchen.

Thinking about second chances, I remember telling Constance about my father. About him making me incontinent with fear. About the slaps. The rage, the shame, the humiliation. My inability to forgive him. About the times I hated myself for catching myself doing to Burt only a moderated version of what my father did to me: the put-downs, the constant latent accusation of being up to something, suspecting him of being bad in some way, lying, selfish, unkind. *She is always up to no good, that one.* The admonitions in front of other people. *She wouldn't know the truth if it was standing in front of her.* The problem with this is well known. You end up living up to these at some point in your life until you realise, one day, if you are lucky, that it wasn't your thing; it was theirs. But you might not. It is a parody– being given a chance at life. It is as if the universe, with its evolutionary magic, says, "I give you a life. But, first, you must resolve the problems left by your parents and theirs. If you don't, well, then you will live a life burdened with their Sisyphus boulder." Talk about giving with one hand and taking away with the other.

Why do you forget some things and not others? And why is forgiving my father so hard for me?

Don and I are sitting in the garden, watching the sun draw inexorably to the point where the sea meets the sky, and although it happens every night, I am mesmerised each time by how fast the sun disappears behind the horizon's line once it sets on its top. There is almost no wind, and the only noise is the cicadas' sonata and dogs in the distant park. The children are at sleepovers, and the night is young. We have a whole evening to do what we please, and it should feel like a gift, but it doesn't. The silent house is making me feel superfluous. There is no one there for Don to demand some peace and quiet while we eat our dinner. No one is arguing, and there is no noise emanating from the TV next door or Burt's gaming device. No one shouts I wish you were never born, or I hate you. I wish I was an only child. Or calling one of us the worst parent ever. It's strange what you can miss.

We used to have so many rows about the "peace and quiet" at the dinner table. But they are children, for God's sake! Yes, they are, and I can ask for a bit of peace and quiet to eat my dinner. It's not unreasonable, M. For fuck sake, Don. From God to fuck in less than three seconds. Kids are not naturally silent. It used to get beaten out of them. And so it would go on until Don would get up and go and eat somewhere else, and the kids and I would sit in silence at the table until one of them would ask Mum are you and Dad going to get divorced.

We haven't yet. It is our 25th wedding anniversary today, and we should make the most of the kids being away, but the problem with shoulds is the expectations they raise and the inevitable disappointment that comes with them not being met. Because it never is just one more story. Or, just one more piece of chocolate. Or, just one more glass of wine. We will always want something just beyond what we get.

I put down my glass of wine, which is silky smooth, and I tell Don I wrote a poem.

'Oh yeah?' He says, not raising his head from his phone.

I want him to look at me.

'Yeah. It's about us.'

'Cool.' He sounds cautious.

He doesn't look at me. He is hiding the pain leftovers from a long time ago. Except some feelings are timeless, they have no sense of time, and they can catch you out. Don is a secret poet. He is better at it than me because he likes to build things according to a set of instructions, and poems are more tightly structured than any other words put together. The sad thing is he only writes when he is sad. The good thing is he only wrote poems at two points in his life. Once, when he was sixteen, his friend died at the rugby pitch, electrocuted by a hose pipe. The second time, when we went through a particularly bad patch. That's what people called it. A bad patch. Like it was a space thing. A patch of dead grass.

'It's a poem for you, really.'

'Ok.'

'I sent it to you.'

'Ok. I will look at it tonight.'

'Ok.' I say. I will have to wait.

'It's a lovely wine, isn't it.' Don says. 'Did someone give it to us?'

And then, as if in response, as if reading my mind, a picture falls off the wall with a loud shattering noise that only a big pane of glass can make so exquisitely. It's like it is saying, is that all you have to say?

Really? The picture is from ten years ago, us with the kids draped around us, toothless smiles and sleepless nights not quite hidden under the camera's eye. Glad to have a good reason to extract myself, I get up to tidy up the glass. It's no good, Don making me feel like I made all the mess back then. We both made it. But I know underneath this thought, it's not him making me feel bad. I am doing it all by myself. Unlike me, Don is a forgiving type. Then the doorbell rings, dogs start barking and Don stands up, his chair making a sound which changes the key of the next interval of this piece. Constance and Elliot have arrived.

It is just an ordinary evening, yet how satiating ordinary can feel. Like a glass of clear cold water on a hot summer's day. It's ordinary, and yet it is all you want in that moment, and the moment couldn't be improved by anything more. I am outside with Constance. We smoke or vape and watch the sky that looks like a glowworm paradise, and neither of us feels like saying anything just now. We had been talking about my first book. Constance is not an avid reader and has finally read it. She said it was beautiful and clever. She became a little tearful, probably just the wine, but I was taken aback by this. I never knew how to react in social situations when people cried. It was different with clients. I always knew how to be with them. This was because of the frame that therapy provides – you never hug them. You always rely on your words and on the silence that can be more containing than any number of words, if you know how to be silent well. Anyway, doubtful of what I was going to do next, if this was what people were supposed to do in the "normal" outside-of-the-therapy-room world, I hugged Constance in an awkward hug. I feel cautious about this because I know that sometimes people don't like to be made to stop crying. Sometimes, if you hug them, they think you can't bear their pain, and they think you want them to stop crying. Sometimes, if you stop them, what they hear is you can't bear their tears. But these were tears for me, even if they were tipsy tears, and I felt bad, even if I felt glad my writing could make people feel things.

Anyway, by the time I stop thinking all of this, Constance stops the tears, and I won't look at her for a while just to give her some privacy. Sometimes, to look is to strip someone. It makes both of us look at the horizon that is showing off in front of us, it didn't care to be stripped at all. Two women and the sea. Only the deep row of trees between us, a master's palette of green and blue now darkened, blended into one by the sky, the distant city lights betraying the line that separates the air and water. I feel at ease with Constance, like you might with someone you have known for a long time. For a moment, then, I feel like I am looking at us both from some other place, standing there, shoulder to shoulder, one child-bearing hip to another, the cigarette smoke merging together in the distance. We are nearly fifty – how did that happen?

We were two women at one end of the Earth. Two women, two mothers, daughters and sisters. Two women who were friends. We were born in the opposite parts of the world. We look different, we sound different, we *are* different, and yet there is something that connects us. Like with Flitwick. It makes me think of my friend in England. I miss her. We all have something that connects us in this crazy gigantic diamond of a universe. I don't know how to put it in words because it doesn't feel like it is a word thing. It feels embodied, like a shared visceral awareness of the edginess of the shaky nature of human relationships, you hold on tight, or you say fuck it, letting go, hoping for the best. The shaky nature of being a human. An unspoken understanding about our proud fragility, about the edge of a reason, and the edge of reasonableness. An understanding that we all live on the edge of a reason. Some too close for comfort, some too far to see it.

My phone pings with a message. It's Don.

"I read the poem. It's lovely. I made some changes to it. It was a terrible part of our lives. It still hurts."

'Don is fixing things again.' I say to Constance as she looks up from her phone.

'Oh yeah?'

Constance says oh yeah, in a number of different ways. Their interpretation ranges from 'Are you ok with it?' to 'That's outrageous'. This way, the hearer can choose which one they prefer, and Constance can happily carry on with the matrix of hypotheses in her head.

'It's a poem I wrote to him.' I say, sticking to the facts because I am not sure if I am ok with it or if it is better.

'Do you want to read it?' Constance asks.

'Do you mind?'

'Nope.' It could be just one letter. That's how fast Constance says it. She is trying to disappear herself into the canvass again, to give me more space. But I have enough.

It doesn't take long for me to read it. *Are you crying, or is it me?* That's how he ends it.

'Do you think we will grow old together?' I ask after a while, coming back from outer space and thinking out loud again.

'Shit, I hope so.' Constance says as if startled by the question.

Constance often does this, looking as if she is startled. But it's just her way of recalibrating that lively brain of hers. 'Do you? Are you planning on moving?'

The question that so many times in my life wasn't even a question. It was more like, when are you? I have lived my life always prepared to move, just in case.

'No.' I say after a moment, 'I don't think I am.' And I think I mean it, but who really knows?

We smile, and Constance says, 'Oh good.' In that same way, as if something was interrupted and took her by surprise.

'Drink?' I say, and we walk in to join our husbands.

EPILOGUE

I am using the knife to cut a piece of home-made wafer my mother made for Hermione. It is the same knife father used to put against my ribs many moons ago, the steely blade worn to a sliver by the passage of time. He is watching me from the chair a few steps away, planted in it with the whole weight of the Parkinsons that was chaining him down like a prisoner. Or a wild dog on a leash.

'Be careful, for god sake, you will break that knife.' He says, suddenly animated, hand raised above his head in a gesture of hopeless disbelief.

I pause for a second, stunned at the absurdity of his words, before returning to the job at hand.

'Did you hear me or what?' threat in the words, emptied by the years, yet still there is a resonance of the tremble of the past. But I have to be brave. This dragon is done with, and he has lost his edge, just like his knife.

'Dad, it's a knife. It will be alright. And if not, we can always get a new one.' Light as a feather, knowing he doesn't want a new one. Sometimes, feathers can be stronger than knives. My father doesn't want new things. What he wants more than anything else is for things to stay as they once were when he was a Scary Dragon.

He shakes his head like it's all futile like I will never understand.

He has felt all his life not understood and not loved and, as a result, never understood or been able to love anyone in return. It's too sad. I feel tears forming at the back of my throat. Not in my eyes. I don't want him to see my pain. I can't let go of this anger; it's a curse. It's his legacy.

'It will be ok, Dad. I promise.' I say.

Once upon a time, in the deep dark forest, right on the edge of the reason, there lived a little girl in the body of an adult. She had to her name a handful of incompatible feelings that constituted the entirety of human nature. Humaneness and cruelty, sadness and joy, love and hate, forgiveness and not. And she was very, very nosy.

THE END

9 781968 966799